HAUNTED SCOTLAND

D0230243

HAUNTED SCOTLAND

Roddy Martine

BIRLINN

First published in 2010 by
Birlinn Limited
West Newington House
10 Newington Road
Edinburgh
EH9 1QS

www.birlinn.co.uk

Copyright © Roddy Martine 2010

The moral right of Roddy Martine to be identified as the author of this work
has been asserted by him in accordance with the Copyright,
Designs and Patents Act 1988

All rights reserved. No part of this publication may be reproduced,
stored or transmitted in any form without the express written
permission of the publisher.

ISBN: 978 1 84158 740 0

British Library Cataloguing-in-Publication Data
A catalogue record for this book is available from the British Library

Typeset by Initial Typesetting Services, Edinburgh
Printed and bound by CPI, Cox & Wyman Ltd, Reading

For Nick and Tania

And in memory of Swein MacDonald,
The Highland Seer (1931–2003)

CONTENTS

ACKNOWLEDGMENTS

The author would like to thank the following for their invaluable help and advice:

Alison Campbell, Ronnie Cox, Elizabeth Fenton-Barnes, Ian Fraser, The Reverend Dr Richard Frazer, Graham Hopner, Martin Hunt, Ewan Irvine, Christopher James, Malcolm and Avril Kirk, Jim and Mary Lamb, Ian Logan, Colin Lindsay McDougal, Alison Milne, Fraser Morrison, Lady Norreys, Luisa Ramazzotti, Paul and Louise Ramsay, John and Carol Steel, Andrew and Helen Murray Thriepland, Jennifer Washington, Gail Young.

My thanks in particular to Hugh Andrew, Andrew Simmons and Kenny Redpath of Birlinn; to Helen Bleck for so methodically copy-editing the text, and, of course, to my agent, John Beaton.

INTRODUCTION

'We Scotch stand ... highest among nations in the matter of grimly illustrating death.'

Robert Louis Stevenson,
Edinburgh: Picturesque Notes (1879)

The writing of *Supernatural Scotland*, my first venture into the realms of the spiritual and paranormal, was an immensely stimulating personal epiphany. Although I had always been intrigued by tales of the inexplicable, I have usually balanced my interest with a healthy dollop of scepticism. Not so much now.

During my research I encountered so many intriguing situations, and so many unlikely sources, that a subconscious pattern soon started to evolve. Almost everyone I interviewed over that period had a story to tell. Two out of every five recalled occurrences that they were logically at a loss to explain and, as I talked to them, I ruthlessly hoovered up their reactions without bias. With so much material to draw upon, it soon became apparent that there was definitely something going on here.

Yet in almost every case there was a universal nervousness as to how friends and families might react. The majority of those I talked to were anxious not to be identified. Ancient taboos and social niceties prevailed. Nobody wanted to be thought of as entirely bonkers.

Then, once *Supernatural Scotland* was published, something rather peculiar began to occur. Associates whom I knew to have deep religious convictions avoided eye contact with me. Strangers started to confide in me as if they felt it safe to trust in my discretion.

The outcome of all of this is *Haunted Scotland*, a compilation of the material I have accumulated over the past five years. Some of the stories have evolved through the mists of time; some of those from the present, in my opinion, are equally unsettling and, probably because of this, some of the characters concerned insisted they remain anonymous.

In the global world of the internet, anything becomes possible. While scientists never cease to astonish us, the more answers they provide, the more questions they pose. I should ask you to bear this in mind as you absorb the contents of this book.

'We shine because we are made of electricity,' announced the New Zealand-born Professor Gerry Gilmore of Cambridge University in the course of a discussion on dark matter with the astrologer Sir Patrick Moore. This observation was made during the 666th episode of the television series *The Sky at Night*. What Professor Gilmore was, in fact, emphasising is that nobody really understands the translucent content of space any more than any of us can begin to comprehend the creation of the universe or the so-called Big Bang theory. Quantum physics accepts the existence of inaccessible parallel universes, but this is still a work in progress. We might like to think that there is a scientific answer for everything, but clearly, as yet, there is not. After centuries of debate, no clear understanding of vitalism, the life force explored in Mary Shelley's epic novel *Frankenstein, or the Modern Prometheus*, has been reached.

Bewildering as this sounds, the majority of us sensibly prefer not to go there. Few of us feel comfortable with the concept of nothingness after death, and therefore many of us welcome anything that gives us some hope of an afterlife.

Surely, our brief existence cannot be all that there is? Given the powers to understand the extent of our lives, there must be some vital purpose in the great scheme of things. For the majority, the answers lie with a belief in God the Creator, the ultimate supernatural force that fills this void. Yet many faiths, while celebrating the divine, remain uncomfortable with the paranormal. Why?

Because simple truths are explicable and therefore easier to subscribe to. So long as planet Earth keeps turning, the death of winter is followed by the rebirth of spring. Everything physical rises out of and reverts back to the compost heap of nature. We know that for fact.

But where does the electricity go? Where does the soul, that sense of existence which is embodied in all human beings, shelter? It would be too trite to introduce the supernatural as the obvious answer at this stage, but let us never forget that manifestations, mostly invisible to the human eye, have been around since the beginning of recorded experience.

Nothing tangible is entirely permanent in the scope of mankind's brief sojourn on this Earth. Global warming, sudden changes in climate temperature, tsunamis, floods, plagues, earthquakes, all natural disasters are integral to the millennial clock and chemical mix of our planet. But who or what primes that engine?

Where does our spark of life come from? Before claiming that a god does not exist, non-believers should first attempt to imagine infinity, then explain why, how and where the universe began, and why, how and where it will end.

The subject is altogether too vast for the average human disposition to comprehend, although it will always remain open to conjecture. Two thousand years or more into mankind's quest for knowledge, and we are still incapable of answering the big questions. Nor are we willing to concede that which we fail to understand: the opening of a door when it was clearly locked; the sound of voices in an empty room; the time-slips of the mind.

There are simply too many cyclical, everyday coincidences for us to be able to dismiss the unexpected as implausible. Being closer to death in their everyday pursuits, our long-ago ancestors, despite their primitive naivety, shared a far greater understanding of such phenomena, and often with a sophistication that leaves us in awe.

They followed the sun, and the moon and the stars at night, as do the tides, the wind, and the seasons. In recognition of this, they created and raised the Callanish Stones on Lewis; the Ring of Brodgar on Orkney; Stonehenge in England; the Stone Circle of Almendres in Portugal; Vottovaara in Russia; the Konark Temple in India, and the giant stone statues on Easter Island in the Pacific Ocean. The list is as infinite as the speculation surrounding them.

The ancients, in their wisdom, had no fear of death; instead, dying was seen only as a change of state, the transition from the physical through the release of the spirit. Accordingly, they paid homage to their ancestors and allowed them to guide them. At the risk of sounding increasingly pretentious, I believe they knew exactly what they were doing. The moment we reject such conduct as mere superstition, we surrender the possibilities. Yet miracles do happen.

In Scotland, land of mountains and big skies, mists and rain, our cities, towns and villages subject to long nights and winter chill, it is too easy to repress the imagination for fear of becoming a laughing stock.

Perhaps that is why the ghosts that we hear about tend generally to be associated with the violent deeds of a distant past.

Scotland's turbulent history certainly provides us with plenty of examples to draw upon, but hauntings are not exclusive to the long ago or to acts of violence. They can relate to relatively mundane incidents as immediate as yesterday. All that is required to glimpse them is a receptive mind. Centuries come and go. Our tenancy in this world is a mere blip in time. Or is it? Are we around for a lot longer than we are encouraged to think?

As with *Supernatural Scotland*, many of those whom I interviewed feared public ridicule. On that basis, I had no option but to promise anonymity. However, there were others, more comfortable in their skins and less susceptible to derision, who had no such reservations. To each and every one I extend my thanks.

1

SHADOWS FROM THE PAST

Behind every man now alive stand thirty ghosts, for that is the ratio by which the dead outnumber the living.

Arthur C. Clarke, *2001: A Space Odyssey* (1968)

All places of antiquity harbour shadows from the past. You have only to acknowledge the relentless passing of the centuries to be aware of the doors opening and closing, and to sense those silent footsteps in the hallway. Whether we like it or not, our mortality is short and transitory. In numbers, the spirits of the departed infinitely outnumber the actuality of the living.

However, that still does not mean that they are at our beck and call. If anything, it makes them all the more elusive, and, although paranormal investigations and ghost festivals have become globally ubiquitous, seldom do they satisfy our insatiable need to believe in an afterlife. Have a look at all of those paranormal databases listed on the internet and you cannot fail to grasp the urgency.

To this end, or should I say beginning, the medium Ewan Irvine has been investigating paranormal phenomena throughout Britain and Ireland for over twenty years. Tall, with ink-black hair and an intense physical presence, he certainly looks the part, and when I was invited to join a group to explore a derelict Edinburgh orphanage known as the Ragged School, it was an opportunity not to be missed.

The Ragged School is situated in Ramsay Lane in the Old Town of Edinburgh, and adjoins the Camera Obscura Outlook Tower, close to the esplanade of Edinburgh Castle. Established in 1847 by Dr Thomas Guthrie, a preacher and reformer, it began by providing food and shelter for up to forty-five of the Old Town's most destitute children. Homeless boys were taught carpentry and how to make shoes, while girls were prepared for a suitable marriage. Dr Guthrie died in 1873, but the Ragged School continued well into the twentieth century, closing after the Second World War. Thereafter, the building lay empty and largely forgotten until the Camera Obscura, itself founded in the Victorian era, was expanded. This would be our last chance to explore the building before the renovation work began.

Ewan Irvine has been aware of his psychic gifts since he was nineteen years old, and, having shaped his abilities as a medium with Portobello Spiritualist Church, set up Full Moon Investigations to participate in the annual Mary King's GhostFest. Mary King, as readers of *Supernatural Scotland* will know, was the inhabitant of a nearby medieval street which was closed off during an outbreak of the bubonic plague during the seventeenth century. The majority of the inhabitants were, we are told, evacuated, but stories persist of those who were left behind, and it is their spirits which are said to haunt the cobbled alleyway which lies forty feet below the quadrangle of today's City Chambers.

There was a veiled moon above us when I joined a team from the Scottish Society of Paranormal Investigation and Analysis and Full Moon Investigations at the top of the High Street. We were a group of around twenty, equipped with torches, cameras, tape recorders, and first-aid kits. Dispersed over the five floors of the Camera Obscura tower, we were invited to make notes of how we felt and to identify hot and cold spots. When I pressed the button of my infra-red thermometer, it initially sprang to 666, then fluctuated between 10 and 19°C. Perhaps I was hallucinating.

Matt from Newcastle was convinced that he saw orbs on the fourth floor, and insisted that there was a moving light in the operations room. Disappointingly, this turned out to be the reflection from some sunglasses one of the spirit guides was using as a headband. But Matt, in his twenties, remained unconvinced.

Various items were set up to record displacement – iron filings, small building blocks, an object coated with flour. As we entered the deserted rooms of the Ragged School, Roberta Gordon, a medium, informed us that she could see a lady whom she felt must have been a past pupil who had returned there to teach. The name Mary sprang to her mind. Ewan Irvine picked up the sound of footsteps pacing the floor, readings from the Scriptures and children's voices on the stair.

'You know that sensation when you enter a room and it either feels right or wrong?' he asked. 'That's what you have to ask yourself. The problem is that a large group like this inevitably disrupts the atmosphere.'

It was now around 2 a.m. and the night air, despite our being indoors, had turned undeniably chilly. The exposed, uneven timbers beneath our feet were bare and covered with a thick dust. The rooms smelt of neglect. The team had set up video equipment to run throughout the night. It looked as though it was going to be a long vigil, and I therefore decided that I had seen enough. Excusing myself, I slipped out of a door and onto the empty, cobbled streets of the Royal Mile to head home.

Time moves on regardless of what we as individuals can do about it. I have no doubt that the spirits of the Ragged School do exist and were, indeed, all about us watching us that night. But I somehow felt guilty for intruding on their silence.

A report of the group's findings appears on the Full Moon Investigations' website (www.fullmooninvestigations.co.uk), but I am not convinced that such forays, while both entertaining and enjoyable, can ever offer convincing proof of the paranormal. Given a fundamental belief in parallel worlds, it is the unexpected, never the mundane, that fires the imagination.

In the summer of 2008, I was on a visit to the Cowal Peninsula with my literary agent John Beaton and his wife Jane, and we had been invited to lunch with Jim and Mary Lamb, who live at Inverchaolain Manse. Among their other guests was their neighbour Bill Caffray, who has exercised his talents as a clairvoyant since childhood.

Having for many years owned a restaurant in Andalucia, Bill returned to Scotland from Spain in 1977 and purchased the Ardfillan Hotel in Dunoon. A resplendent figure in a white suit, he told me how he had found himself rapidly filling a void, his powers of second sight being much in demand.

One summons, for example, had been from Dunans Castle in Glendaruel, the former headquarters of the Fletcher Clan. The Fletchers had relocated from north of Bridge of Orchy as early as 1745, but in 1999, their dramatic Franco-baronial castle was sold to Robert and Ewa Lucas-Gardiner.

The Lucas-Gardiners had already purchased the Manor of Marr, a feudal barony which entitled them to call themselves Lord and Lady Marr. Dunans Castle they transformed into a luxury hotel and once everything was up and running, Lady Marr had called upon Bill to conduct a seance for her.

'I told her I could see her surrounded by people with shaven heads,' he recalled in all sincerity. 'I also warned her that I saw danger if she and her husband remained at the castle.

Of course, that was the last thing either of them wanted to hear.'

A few months after the seance a fire destroyed the first and second floors, forcing the Marrs and twelve other occupants to escape to safety in the early hours of a Sunday morning. The damage was considerable, but mercifully nobody was hurt.

'I try to approach spiritual matters from a logical perspective,' Bill reassured me. 'But with the gift come responsibilities. Nobody can change fate. All of the decisions that affect us have been made long before we got here. I simply tell people what I see. I leave them to come to their own conclusions.'

Mary Lamb, our hostess at Inverchaolain Manse, is Secretary of the Clan Lamont Society, and, after lunch, she took us to see Knockdow House, a mid-fifteenth-century mansion house which, until the late 1950s, had been owned by the Lamont family. The last of the Lamont line at Knockdow was Augusta, who inherited the estate from her unmarried brother Norman. It appears she was most definitely a woman of independent mind.

Having inherited money from her grandmother, she had enrolled herself at Edinburgh University, subsequently becoming an eminent zoologist. Her father, known to be a bit of a tyrant, was horrified. A woman's place was in the marital bed, he fumed. No doubt this was why Augusta remained a spinster for the rest of her life.

When Augusta died, she bequeathed Knockdow to the Clan Lamont Society, which for financial reasons was unfortunately unable to take on the responsibility. For a while the estate passed to Augusta's next of kin, but it was eventually sold in 1990 and has since remained unoccupied.

Before that, however, Bill remembered wonderful cricket matches on the lawn and formal dances taking place in the hall beneath its circular gallery. 'For me Knockdow has always had a really good feel about it,' he said. 'That's why Augusta has never wanted to leave.'

Although he had never known her during her lifetime, Bill told me he had once stepped into the kitchen at Knockdow House and encountered an elderly woman with two younger companions, one slim, the other rather more plump. 'Of course, nobody else could see them, but they were as clear to me as you are now,' he insisted. 'I had no idea who they were at the time, but when I described them afterwards to somebody who had once worked at the house, she immediately identified the older woman as Miss Lamont. The younger ones were kitchen staff. The description I gave of them fitted perfectly.'

Needless to say, there was no sign of Augusta or her maids when our little party toured Knockdow House, but all of the time we were there, Bill seemed anxious to give me a 'transfer', to see if there were any spirits present. For a moment his face glazed over in preparation to enter a trance but, having had no previous connection with either the house or Lamont family, I firmly declined his offer.

So far as I was concerned, if Augusta wished to introduce herself to me she would do so on her own terms and when it suited her.

'She really loved Knockdow,' said Mary Lamb. 'All she really wanted towards the end of her life was to know it would be looked after.'

'There's nothing to be worried about here,' added Bill. 'But isn't it good to know she's still keeping an eye on things?'

2

STONE TAPES

'For who can wonder that man should feel a vague belief in tales of disembodied spirits wandering through those places which they once dearly affected, when he himself, scarcely less separated from his old world than they, is for ever lingering upon past emotions and bygone times, and hovering, the ghost of his former self, about the places and people that warmed his heart of old?'

Charles Dickens, *Master Humphrey's Clock* (1841)

It was during the Perthshire Open Studios Week of 2008 that I first encountered Gordon McNeill-Wilkie. In his everyday existence Gordon is a specialist in dry-stone walls and garden features such as the monumental stone sofa-bench on show at Lethendy House where his partner, the painter Luisa Ramazzotti, was exhibiting her oil portraits.

When I mentioned I was in the process of writing this book, he casually informed me that he was both a faith healer and an exorcist. Slim, with intense blue eyes, he further indicated that he was willing to talk to me openly on the subject. Having found others similarly blessed reluctant to do so, I naturally jumped at the opportunity.

'Such gifts are easily misunderstood, but if you worry about what people think of you then they own you,' he said wisely. 'It's certainly not been easy for me, but once I learned to accept my situation, everything fell into place.'

Gordon was born in 1960 and grew up in Perthshire, where his father was the manager of the Green Hotel at Kinross. 'When I was very young, I used to have nightmares full of sights and sounds and smells,' he explained. 'I often experienced the sensation of leaving my body and flying, and I vividly remember trying desperately to maintain my concentration in case I fell.'

As he grew older, he struggled to shut these thoughts out of his consciousness, but, playing in the woods on the banks of Loch Leven, he was continually aware of the energies surrounding the plants, the trees and the people he encountered. In an attempt to suppress such feelings he turned to macho pursuits such as martial arts. He married and joined the army, enlisting in 15 Para (Scottish Battalion) based at Yorkhill in Glasgow. But when his best friend was killed in front of him in an accident, it affected him deeply.

Shortly after this terrible experience, Gordon met a psychic who gave him a tarot reading in which the death card appeared again and again. She told him not to worry about this, but within months his wife had also died.

Understandably traumatised, Gordon began reading every book he could find relating to the occult and spiritualism, but none provided him with the answers he needed.

That was over twenty-one years ago and when Gordon remarried, he and his second wife moved to live at Bankfoot, where his elderly neighbour, as it transpired, was a practising Buddhist. One day this man, whom he liked enormously, came to see Gordon and confided in him that he had been diagnosed with a serious medical condition. Gordon was intensely shocked, but became even more perplexed when the man said to him, 'I'm a healer, but I can't heal myself. Will you help me?'

At first, Gordon was speechless, but the man went on to explain to him that he had recognised the healing ability in him. 'It's not something you do; it's what you are,' he explained. 'It's not a skill you acquire; you are born with it.'

After some initial hesitation, Gordon placed his hands over the old man's lower back and felt a trembling sensation. After five minutes, he was told to stop.

'That's it gone now,' said the man gratefully, and walked off saying, 'Now you know. This is what you can do.' He was later diagnosed as having fully recovered.

'I felt a huge surge of emotion after that,' said Gordon. 'I'd recently read *Conversations with God*, three books by Neale Donald Walsch. In my head I kept hearing the words, "If there were any gift that I could give you, it would be fearlessness." I knew I had to take myself seriously.'

To start off with, of course, there were doubts. Was it just a case of feeding his own ego? Finally, Gordon decided that he had no choice. He had to do something about it, and told himself everything was possible. He wanted the full party pack. As Jesus said, 'These things I have done, so ye will do also.'

Ironically, all of this was going on just as Gordon's life was once again starting to fall apart. Remarried, with three young children, his marriage failed.

'Everything was going wrong for me. I even had my car stolen,' he told me. 'I moved to live at Inver, near Dunkeld, and having nowhere to go in the evenings but the pub, I soon found myself healing some of the locals. I got a job as a personal trainer at the Dunkeld Hilton, and then a chiropractor friend suggested I open a clinic.' Gordon had previously not considered himself to be an exorcist, but soon found that people were coming to him with psychological problems. This was compounded when a white witch, whose name he prefers to withhold out of respect for her privacy, came to see him from Edinburgh and regressed him.

'Afterwards, she became my mentor,' he said. 'She made me understand that I was not a source, but a conduit. In this game your biggest enemy is your ego.

'The human soul is huge,' he continued disarmingly. 'It contains the body, not the other way around. Every lifetime is burned into your soul's memory bank. You take this information (which can be accessed) with you from lifetime to lifetime.'

Gordon does not believe in the Devil, as such, but he does acknowledge the existence of evil spirits and demons. One of his more memorable exploits was when he was asked to clear the interiors and grounds of Ashintully Castle, near Blairgowrie.

'I came across a group of spirit witches, or medicine women, as I prefer to call them, and moved them away from the old mausoleum,' he recalls. 'I thought nothing of it at the time, but on the road home in the car I found myself looking over my shoulder all the time, as if there were passengers in the back seat.'

At home in their sitting room that night, he and Luisa were seated at opposite ends of a sofa, when the cushion between them compressed and the room turned bitterly cold.

'My knees were freezing and I began to wonder what we had brought home with us,' he recalled.

Then the shadow of a girl with very black hair materialised at Luisa's feet, with yet another woman, presumably the girl's mother, standing directly in front of them saying:

'An' fit are ye gonnae dae noo ye've cleared the hoose an' cleared the chepel? Fit ye gonnae dae wi' us?'

'There was no sense of a threat,' said Gordon. 'I knew immediately that they were in that rut where there is no concept of time, so I explained very gently to them what I had done and told them that I could help them to go to a better place.'

'Mebbe we'll just stay here,' the older woman responded.

'Both were frightened by what they'd been told about Hell,' he explained. 'You would be too if you'd spent all of your mortal existence being persecuted. So I was just wondering what I should do next, when a ray of brilliant white light showed through the window. Instantly, the daughter stood up and was carried away. Instantaneously, the mother leaned forward to give me an icy hug and off she went too. It was really very extraordinary and the room then warmed up.' A year later, Gordon was asked to return to the castle to clear the dungeon.

'During that first clearance I knew I was out of my depth,' he mused when retelling me the story. 'This time it was different.'

The dungeon lay under the castle and, being below water level, the vaults had been regularly flooded. Gordon had also been told that in medieval times prisoners were frequently put there to drown.

'This time I felt much more confident about what I was going to do,' he said. 'The dungeon entrance lay below a hatch on the ground floor, and, as I entered the hallway, all of the dogs belonging to the castle started rushing around and barking in a frenzy. I began by opening the windows and, as I raised the hatch and peered into the space below, a piece of citrine I'd placed in my shirt pocket fell into the void. It had an unexpectedly calming effect. The next thing I knew, I was lowering myself through the opening.

'The first thing I noticed was the fetid air. Next, I felt my throat being squeezed, but this is quite a common occurrence in such circumstances. I knew that whoever it was that was doing this, would stop as soon as I'd completed the clearance.'

Gordon revealed that a lot of what he does involves procedures, prayers and rituals which to those of a cynical disposition might appear a trifle absurd. 'This is because you have to convince whatever it is that you are up against that you mean business. Coming from the past, they understand rituals.'

He had therefore taken with him a replica Japanese ceremonial sword made of steel and embossed with a gold dragon, and he boldly called out, 'Begone foul evil spirits all, this is my word so heed the call!'

Immediately the energy in the dungeon shifted. In the very same instant, Carol, the lady of the house, who was standing in the room above, witnessed nine black shapes fly out of the hatch and evaporate through a window towards the light.

'It gave her quite a shock!' said Gordon. 'But at least she knew I was doing my job!'

Gordon was adamant about differentiating between ghosts and what he called 'stone tapes'. His theory was that in every old building where negative events take place, energies are absorbed electromagnetically into the stone, and these energies can be replayed. 'When, for example, somebody sees an apparition pass through a wall, it's not a ghost at all, it's a stone recording,' he insisted. Both good and evil spirits have the means to interact with human beings. A ghost, even when it has been shown the light, is able to come and go as it pleases, whereas a stone tape is a hologram, nothing more. He went on to explain that if somebody dies in a state of imbalance, they will pass over, while some of their negative traits may possibly remain behind. These can attach themselves to the living. 'Sometimes when people experience mood swings, it can be because this negativity has latched onto them. That's where an exorcist needs to step in.'

Whenever Gordon gives a consultation, he previously aligns his operational space with crystals for protection. 'It's important that clients are welcomed into a comfortably furnished room,' he says. 'But hidden in the system there are things to protect them, me and the house.'

To help him, he makes use of obsidian, lapus lazuli, rose quartz, good for balancing the emotions, and citrine, the 'stone of the divine', which has four main functions – it 'absorbs, transmutes, dissipates, and grounds negative energy'.

When Gordon volunteered to give me what he calls a 'Wash Down', he had me first remove my shoes and wristwatch. Watches, he explained, absorb the bad experiences of life. If you have worn a watch for a period of years, it is a good thing to have it cleansed.

The Wash Down itself is a process by which he claims somebody is introduced to their full potential. It involved me clasping a piece of angelite in my right hand and a piece of lapis lazuli in my left. Having relaxed in a vintage Parker Knoll chair covered with a white cloth, I was instructed to close my eyes. In the background, I listened to a soundtrack of Enya, while Gordon enunciated various prayers.

The Wash Down took a fleeting four minutes. To be honest, I found it both relaxing and enervating in equal measure, creating an inner sense of calm which surprised me. In my analytical state of mind, I had not expected that. Moreover, I was introduced to my spirit guide who, I was told, would become responsible for my future wellbeing.

'You are now empowered to fulfil all of your innermost wishes,' said Gordon.

As I drove home that night I somehow found this extremely reassuring.

3

SECOND SIGHT

It would be a gain to the country were it vastly more superstitious, more bigoted, more gloomy, more fierce in its religion than at present it shows itself to be.

Cardinal Newman, 'History of my
Religious Opinions from 1833 to 1839'
in *Apologia Pro Vita Sua* (1865)

My grandmother was the seventh child of a seventh child, which in the Celtic tradition made her fey or psychic, and there is a story in the family (as I am sure exists in every Scots family) that one night she had a dream in which a childhood friend came to her bedside to say goodbye. On coming to consciousness, she immediately awoke her disgruntled husband to tell him about this. The next day a telegram arrived to confirm that their friend had died in the night.

Second sight is infinitely more closely allied to the Celts than to any other race, although it also occurs in tribes of Red Indians, and in the folklore of Australian Aboriginals and the Maoris of New Zealand. Why Scots and Irish should specifically be singled out for the gift might suggest some sort of unique genetic provenance buried deep within their Celtic birthright.

Premonitions are commonplace throughout Scotland's long and lawless story. As early as the twelfth century, Thomas of Ercildoun predicted the union of Scotland with England; in 1388, the second earl of Douglas dreamed of his own death before the Battle of Otterburn; in 1513, a ghostly spectre seen at the Mercat Cross in Edinburgh warned of the impending catastrophe at Flodden.

In *Supernatural Scotland*, I wrote of my friend Swein MacDonald of Ardgay, in Sutherland. Swein died at the age of seventy-one in 2003. He too was possessed of the Highland gift of second sight, warning of the 1993 Braer oilfield spill on Shetland only days before it occurred. With Swein, all of the clichés were in place. He was a seventh son born on the seventh day of the seventh month. He predicted the marriage of the Prince of Wales to Lady Diana Spencer, the birth of Prince William within a year of their wedding, and the subsequent break-up of their marriage.

A portly, red-faced crofter with a shock of white beard, Swein enjoyed his whisky and there was a childlike naivety about him. I visited him whenever I found myself in the vicinity of his smallholding overlooking the Dornoch Firth, and always came away with the conclusion that he was as baffled by his powers as were the rest of us. Swein's predictions were simplistic, but touched a chord. His readings, as he called them, were calculated to reassure rather than to disturb. In the bar of a local hotel he was denounced by a stranger who called him a crook and a fantasist. Swein responded by warning him to be careful what he said because in a year's time he would have no shoes. A month later, this same individual was driving towards Tain when his car collided head-on with another vehicle. The unfortunate man spent the ensuing three years of his life in a wheelchair.

But there was no malice about Swein. Often he totally failed to comprehend the significance of what he predicted. On more than one occasion he told me that he found the burden of his gift deeply troubling.

Another such individual with an extraordinary gift was Henry Torrance, whom I had been sent to for advice when researching a project on the Knights Templar. He was immensely knowledgeable on matters both spiritual and occult, and we rapidly embarked upon a firm friendship, to the extent that I would occasionally invite him to accompany me when I went on excursions.

On one occasion, we had driven to have lunch with a mutual friend in Innerleithen and we were passing through the village of Clovenfords, west of Galashiels, when Henry requested I pull over to the side of the road. There was an urgency in his voice and I was concerned. He was elderly. At first I thought he had been taken ill.

'Can't you see them?' he asked in an agitated voice.

'Who?' I replied.

'There, in that field. Those poor children.'

I looked across the fence towards a copse beside the Caddon Water. The sun shone hazily, but the enclosure of trees at the water's edge appeared gloomy, in dark shadow. So far as I could see, there was nobody there.

'They look so sad,' continued my old friend. 'So frightened.'

'But I can't see anybody,' I protested.

He looked disappointed. This was most unlike him. A man of substance in that he weighed around twenty stone, Henry was used to being in control.

'You probably think I'm mad,' he said reproachfully after a pause. 'But I can assure you they are there. Clear as daylight. But it seems I'm the only one who can see them.'

We had had a similar conversation once before when he had asked me if I believed in faith healing. A retired Edinburgh banker, survivor of a German prisoner-of-war camp during the Second World War and awarded a Military Cross, Henry was not somebody one might expect to be preoccupied with the occult. But he was perfectly serious.

Ever since his childhood, he confessed to me, he had seen things that nobody else was aware of.

'At first I thought it was perfectly normal,' he said. 'It never occurred to me that it was a gift or a curse, or whatever you want to call it. It doesn't happen very often, but sometimes I'm somewhere I haven't been before and I know something is wrong. That's when they appear, figures from the past, or at least, that's what I assume them to be, almost as if they're wanting to tell me something. What should I do? I can't ignore them. They don't mean me any harm. Quite the opposite, in fact. They need help. That's why I became interested in faith healing in the hope of finding out what I can do for them.'

Poor Henry. His thirty-eight-year marriage had ended in separation and a painful divorce. Increasingly, those close to him regarded him with amused tolerance. He was harmless, they told me.

'Don't pay any attention to him if he turns all silly,' his son insisted, when I mentioned I had seen his father on the steps of the Edinburgh College of Parapsychology.

But I did not consider him silly. I was intrigued, and often looked in on his Bruntsfield flat for a chat and a coffee. On this occasion, I had volunteered to drive him to Walkerburn for lunch with some mutual friends.

'Please don't say anything about this when we get there,' he pleaded. 'They already think I'm a bit dotty. I'm so sorry. I shouldn't have asked you to stop. I just needed to have a proper look at those poor people.'

He was courteous and kind, and I was curious. 'What did they look like?' I asked.

He closed his eyes as we set off again. 'There were at least a dozen women with several children, four or five maybe, all pretty emaciated. Their clothes were ragged and grubby. They looked half-starved.'

Nothing more was said on the subject. We had an amusing lunch with our friends where, so far as I can recall, the conversation centred on labrador puppies. I drove Henry home afterwards and, having delivered him to his door, promptly forgot all about the incident, that is until three months later, when I ran into him by chance.

I was walking along Melville Crescent when he hailed me and strode purposefully towards me with his hand outstretched. 'I just wanted to let you know I finally got to the bottom of those wretched people we saw when you drove me to lunch with George and Helen,' he said.

'You saw,' I corrected him.

'Yes. Well, at least you didn't appear to think I was entirely potty. At least, I hope not.'

I nodded. 'I always keep an open mind,' I said.

'And so you should. If only others followed your example,' he said with a sigh of resignation. 'Anyway, let me tell you what it was all about.'

On returning to Edinburgh, Henry had immediately telephoned his close confidant Marion McNaught to ask her advice. A well-respected historian, Marion was used to such enquiries and having confirmed a map reference, began a search. Timeslips, for that is what this must have been, occur throughout and across the centuries, visible only to those susceptible to them, and on the spot where they took place. Before long she had come up with an explanation.

Enclosed within an envelope of rolling hills, there was once, long, long ago, a small encampment at Caddonlee. It was a simple life in that era, safe from the intrusion of the outside world, or so it was thought. All about was lush pasture land. The local community had their own livestock and were blessed with a plentiful supply of water from the River Tweed. They kept themselves to themselves. With no roads or even footpaths, strangers rarely strayed into their territory.

But alas, nobody noticed the Roman soldiers until they were upon them. Sent on a punitive mission to suppress the hostile elements of the locality, no questions were asked. It was slaughter on sight. That day the river ran red with blood and the corpses of the innocent; slaughtered men were left to rot where they dropped.

Further down the glen a group of women were tending to their chores with their children. Hearing distant cries they had at first assumed that it was their menfolk rounding up the cattle. It was only when they returned to the village at sunset that the full extent of the devastation became apparent. At this juncture, they too were set upon by the legionnaires and put to the sword.

'Souls caught in limbo almost always belong to those who have met with a violent or unhappy end,' explained Henry. 'All those emotions – anger, frustration, despair – create a void in which departed spirits become lost, sometimes for centuries. All that those poor people wanted me to do was to help them to find their way to the light.' He went on to tell me that he and Marion had returned to the river bank with a Bible and spent the afternoon in prayer. After a while, the prevailing sense of gloom had dispersed and a warm sun touched their faces. 'After all those centuries I was able to show them the light,' said Henry with satisfaction. 'It enabled them to pass over to a better place.'

Henry died peacefully in his sleep four years ago at the age of ninety-two, but every time I drive along the A72 between Galashiels and Walkerburn, I think of him.

4

AN AWAKENING

Two orders of being, the visible and the invisible, pause on the doorstep of this grey hour, and which is going to advance upon you you hardly know.

Neil Miller Gunn, *The Other Landscape* (1954)

As was emphasised by Gordon McNeill-Wilkie in Chapter Two, the gift of clairvoyance can become a curse. It takes courage to come to terms with it and to lower the barriers. Nobody enjoys being made fun of. Nor does anyone relish being accused of self-delusion.

Joan Charles has worked in personal and intuitive development for over twenty-five years. A cheery, stylishly dressed personality with bobbed blond hair, she is a regular contributor to lifestyle magazines, writing on such subjects as intuition, self-discovery and psychic awareness. Based in the town of Gourock, where she was born, her own self-awareness began when she was seven years old and she found herself looking into a mirror as if from outside herself.

'I didn't have a clue what it was all about,' she protested. 'I was a very timorous and highly strung child. I simply didn't understand the sensations that I was experiencing. There was no one to help me so I decided to put whatever it was on hold until I was eleven.'

Joan remembered going home from school over her lunch break one day to walk the family dog. When she arrived at the front door, she heard somebody calling out her name, yet there was nobody in the house. The voices continued until she was twenty-four, by which time her mother had died of cancer and Joan was married with four children. Around this time she and her husband separated, but she insists that the voices were not the only pressures on their relationship. 'It was not the best of marriages,' she recalled regretfully.

However, it was only after her marriage had come to an end that she summoned up the courage to start visiting 'spirit churches'. Her next move was to buy herself a book on tarot reading. 'I knew almost at once that I didn't need a book,' she said. 'I could manage very well without one.'

And it was this realisation that persuaded her to become involved with alternative therapies. For a time she worked in a health clinic, and several of her clients remained with her when she set up on her own after it closed down. 'I started to give readings to audiences in Glasgow,' she explained.

Soon afterwards, she was approached by an agent who suggested she put together a stage act. Almost before she knew it, she was performing in pubs and clubs, which in turn led to her running corporate courses on intuitive leadership and being signed up to write a column on star signs in the *Sunday Post*.

Training groups in team-building, self-belief, awareness and intuition came easily to Joan, especially when engaging with children. 'Once people open themselves up to the possibilities available to them, they become infinitely more confident in their own powers. I learned that lesson very early on in my own life.

But you have to be prepared for every kind of eventuality. Things may not always turn out the way you want them to.'

She remembered one reading in particular. A girl came to ask her for advice, and Joan told her that she could see black bin bags stuffed full of money. It had something to do with the girl's husband. The girl was startled and alarmed by this, and told Joan defensively that her husband worked for the local brewery, and had been given the money by his boss.

Joan had then informed the girl that she saw the money being transferred into a series of Tesco carrier bags, and that a body would be found floating in the River Clyde.

'The girl was horrified,' said Joan. 'She turned completely white and left in a panic. I never heard from her again, but I can't help what comes to me when I do a reading. I only hope she managed to sort things out.'

Joan remained silent while she thought about this. 'Everything flashes before you in your mind's eye,' she continued solemnly. 'Sometimes I feel like an interpreter for the dumb. It's not that simple either way. I certainly don't claim to have all the answers. You have to look for symbols, and you try to do your best to work out what's going on, but sometimes it is impossible to translate what you see into making sense. It's often very stressful.'

However, calling in a medium can definitely solve problems, as Jacqueline Heriot can confirm. I was in St Andrews and had arranged to meet her in the St Andrews Castle Visitor Centre, where, as one might expect, the past confronts the present in this old university town with dramatic impact.

But the castle ghosts were not what Jacqueline wanted to talk to me about, at least not to start off with. 'I've always believed in serendipity,' she began vaguely. 'If you are really genuinely interested in something, information comes to you.'

Having returned from South Africa to live in Scotland some years earlier, Jacqueline had at first moved into a house at Strathkinness, close to St Andrews, but when some friends put their former spinner's cottage in the village of Ceres up for sale, she decided to make them an offer. Much to her delight, it was accepted.

'Ceres is a really pretty place with a village green,' she said. 'The people who live there really take care of their houses.'

Once Jacqueline's offer was accepted, her friends invited her over to celebrate with a bottle of champagne. 'I was overjoyed,' she said.

That was certainly true at the time, but the sense of euphoria did not last for long. As she lay in bed on her very first night under the cottage roof, she felt her face being gently stroked.

'It felt like someone's breath,' she recalled, shivering. 'At first I thought I must be imagining it, but after that first night it became a regular occurrence. It was almost as if somebody had climbed into bed with me. Night after night, I'd just lie there, waiting for it to happen again.

'I use candles a lot,' she added. 'I particularly like tea lights, and one morning as I was clearing up in my bedroom before going to work, I dropped several used ones into the wastepaper basket. Of course, it was a wicker basket, so all the soot filtered through the bottom and onto my white carpet. It was so annoying. I tried to clean it up with carpet cleaner, but that simply made it worse with dirty streaks, so I decided to leave it until later.'

But when Jacqueline returned home that evening, she was astonished. The carpet was pristine white and there was no sign of the stains. 'I can remember thinking, that's great,' she recalled, 'the carpet cleaner must have worked.'

Nevertheless, the sleepless nights continued and they soon began to take their toll on her.

'When I went into work I'd apologise to my boss, saying that

I wasn't functioning properly. I'd hardly slept for about two months. I used to leave the bedside light on all night, but that only made it more difficult to sleep. It was probably something to do with the strain I was under, but my back started to play up. I thought I was managing it, but then as I was trying to fall sleep one night, I felt this strange rubbing sensation, as if somebody or something was pressing into the small of my back.'

Not long after this, Jacqueline was sitting on her bed using her mobile phone to send a text message when her legs were pulled from under her and she felt herself being pushed onto the floor.

'That was too much,' she complained. 'I shouted out loud that I didn't mind whoever it was being there, but they had to leave me alone as I had to work for a living. Otherwise, I'd have to leave!'

By then, Jacqueline had become a tour guide for Historic Scotland at St Andrews Castle and, aware of her worsening predicament, one of her colleagues produced a newspaper article about Brion Keppie, a Bathgate-based psychic.

'So I telephoned him,' said Jacqueline. 'I told him that I thought that there was a presence in my home, and he came to see me.'

Brion wore a striped business suit and glasses and carried a briefcase, which was not at all what Jacqueline had expected. He nevertheless set about his work.

To begin with, he said he felt nothing untoward about the atmosphere in the rooms, but, as soon as he entered Jacqueline's bedroom, the mood changed.

'He's given me his name,' Brion told her. 'He's called James Macpherson. A long time ago he worked as a porter on the coach and horses which used to travel through the village. He says they used to stop off to see the folk who lived here at the time. He's only back to visit old friends.'

Brion concentrated further. 'Now he's showing me symbols of travelling trunks and a sailor's haversack, which suggests that he's leaving. He's telling me that he cleaned your carpet for you. He doesn't want you to leave because he remembers how happy you were that first night when you came here to drink champagne with your friends. He says he's sorry for making you fall off your bed. He says he was bored.'

The invisible dialogue continued, with Macpherson telling Brion that he was not a regular caller; that it might be another thirty years before he returned. At this point, Brion turned abruptly to Jacqueline and asked who it was that played bingo?

Jacqueline was mystified. 'Bingo? Nobody I know plays bingo!' she protested.

'But somebody must,' said Brion. 'I'm having bingo tokens thrown at me. I can see word counters and an elderly lady. Is it your grandmother?'

'It was then that I remembered,' Jacqueline told me. 'When I was a child, my paternal grandmother regularly came to visit me with a cousin of about my own age. She'd bring a bingo game to occupy us. Nobody else could have known about that.'

'It's because of your back,' Brion informed her. 'Your grandmother says she is sorry if she frightened you the other night when she came into your bed. She was only trying to send you warmth. It had nothing to do with Mr Macpherson!'

'It was altogether extraordinary,' confessed Jacqueline. 'I certainly hadn't told him that I'd hurt my back.'

Although the outcome of Brion's exorcism was that Jacqueline's mind was eventually put at rest, she did eventually sell the cottage and has since returned to live in Strathkinness. And she still works for Historic Scotland at St Andrews Castle.

Searching the internet, I have found no fewer than eight clairvoyants listed in Scotland under the umbrella of UK Psychics.

They range from tarot readers and astronomers in Kirkwall and Aberdeen to the Christian Spiritualist Church in Bathgate.

This latter intrigued me, so I telephoned the number given and spoke to the Reverend Mhairi Derby-Pitt, who told me that the Bathgate Christian Spiritualist Church was founded in 1946 by Charlotte Whelan, her grandmother. Charlotte, according to the Reverend Mhairi, was an extraordinary and remarkable woman who, rather spectacularly, was the seventh child of a seventh child of a seventh child.

'I was brought up on Christian Spiritualism,' explained the Reverend Mhairi, who, with her father, the Reverend Bernard Brian Derby-Pitt, today oversees a congregation of around 300. 'What you have always to remember as a pastor is that you have a duty of care,' she says firmly.

The Reverend Mhairi and her father are both fully ordained as ministers, which qualifies them to conduct legal marriages. I found this fascinating as, up until then, I had been unaware that virtually anyone can legally be ordained as a minister providing they are in some way affiliated to a church. In America, you can even be ordained online.

However, the Reverend Mhairi is also fully qualified as a 'Spiritual, Aura, Colour and Crystal Healer and Trainer' and is registered with the Greater World and Institute of Spiritualist mediums.

'I've been operating as a medium since I was twelve years old,' she told me. 'I've walked and talked with spirits all of my life.'

And such powers, it transpires, have even involved a spot of private detective work. Up until shortly before I spoke to her she had been working closely on the Peter Manuel murder case with author Hector MacLeod.[1]

---

[1] *Peter Manuel, Serial Killer*, Hector MacLeod and Malcolm McLeod, Mainstream, 2009.

Manuel, an American-born serial killer, is known to have murdered seven people in Lanarkshire and southern Scotland between 1956 and his arrest in January 1958. Six months later, he was the second last person to be hanged in HM Prison Barlinnie. It was yet another dark and shocking episode in the history of Scottish crime.

'It's hard to understand why people do bad things,' says the Reverend Mhairi. 'My father and I have been consulted on a number of murder cases. They are always particularly difficult to deal with because there is so much emotion involved with those who have lost loved ones.'

5

MULTIPLE OCCUPANCY

The ghost that got into our house on the night of
November 17, 1915, raised such a hullabaloo of mis-
understandings that I am sorry I didn't just let it keep
on walking, and go to bed.

James Thurber, *My Life and Hard Times* (1933)

The concept of time racing behind and ahead of us is far from being
a twenty-first-century anomaly. From the puzzles of Leonardo Da
Vinci to the notional machinations of novelist HG Wells and the
recent television series *FlashForward*, based on Robert J Sawyer's
novel, mankind has eagerly grasped at the prospect of revisiting
the past and controlling the future. Yet when the past goes so far
as to stand up boldly in front of us, our basic instinct is to dismiss
what we see as a trick of the mind.

Given that astronomers are capable of analysing the past by
peering into the outer layers of the universe light years away, why
should it be so very peculiar for the rest of us to catch glimpses of
people and events from another age when time occasionally turns in
on itself? Perhaps the fundamental problem is that those other ages
are already generously documented in stone and print, or caught in
sound or on film, making it hard for us to take holograms seriously.

So we make light of our fantasies, attributing them to a hyper-active mindset and this, in turn, encourages our innermost terrors to surface before we can think them through.

In his first term at Heriot Watt University, Adrian Shaw, then aged twenty, found himself sharing accommodation with Fin Armstrong, a fellow student from Northern Ireland. The room allocated to them was on the first floor of a Victorian tenement in Johnston Terrace, which in turn faces the Tolbooth St John's Highland Church, today the headquarters of the Edinburgh International Festival Society.

'Our flat was above an office belonging to Edinburgh Council,' recalled Adrian. 'The building backed onto the recently opened Witchery Restaurant, and the windows to the rear looked over the roofs of the West Bow.'

Although both lads were from Northern Ireland, Adrian had not known Fin previously but described him as a very typical Ulster Protestant from County Armagh. 'His family were devout church-goers and very rigid in their commitment to their faith.'

To begin with, the two students were wholly preoccupied with settling into academic life, attending lectures, hanging out in bars and making new friends, but it soon became apparent to Adrian that Fin had a darker side.

'With that dour Irish accent, he would sometimes talk about seeing dead people in the street,' said Adrian. 'It all became a bit creepy.'

They were sharing a room with two single beds, and, shortly after they moved in, they started to hear strange noises in the night. 'It was as if somebody had walked into our room and we could hear them sitting down heavily. But there was nobody there.'

This went on for weeks. Then one night Fin announced that he thought he could see something. When Adrian asked him what it looked like, he said that whatever it was appeared to be very tall, but he could only make out the outline. It was one-dimensional.

Adrian was beginning to find all of this a trifle unnerving when events reached a climax.

'As usual, I was half-asleep when the door to the room opened and I thought I heard something or somebody enter,' he said. 'I sat up in bed and listened hard. Whoever, or whatever, it was, was walking around the room in a circle. Then I sensed a heavy weight sitting down on the end of my mattress.

And this time I could hear heavy breathing and smell its breath, sickly and putrid. The next moment I heard Fin calling out to me urgently from across the room telling me I really needed to get out of my bed.

'When I turned on the light I could see Fin sitting up in his bed and looking petrified,' recalled Adrian. 'Needless to say, I was out from under my blankets in a flash, and when I asked him what he had seen, he said that whatever it was had had the body of a man, but the head of a dog. If it hadn't been so real, I'd have laughed out loud.' The very next day, he and Fin began looking for somewhere else to live.

'No, we definitely weren't on drugs,' insisted Adrian firmly. 'Neither of us was into that.'

For a while they wondered if it might have had something to do with being so close to Castle Hill, where all those witches were burned at the stake in the sixteenth century. They also went to the library to try and identify what Fin thought he had seen, but the closest thing they could find was a cynocephalus, a drawing of Saint Christopher with the head of an Egyptian dog.

'I know it sounds ridiculous, but when you've been through something like that you become desperate for answers,' said Adrian.

'Cynocophali are associated with pagan religions, but why one should have been lurking in our Edinburgh flat is anyone's guess. Something horrible must have happened there some time in the past.'

Johnston Terrace, coiling up the southern slope of the Castle Rock, with the Grassmarket below, culminates in a row of tenements where Castle Hill meets the Royal Mile. On the street front is an eclectic selection of shops, but in the dwelling spaces above are lodgings through which generations of tenants have passed.

Knowing Adrian not to be prone to flights of fantasy, I was intrigued and decided to investigate the matter further. At first it seemed an impossible task, but, undaunted, I spent a couple of days scrolling through rolls of microfilm in the records department of the Central Library and, much to my amazement, finally came up with a confidential cases record which somehow made everything fall into place.

It was a sad little story and the outcome was unsatisfactory in that, in an age lacking in forensic knowledge, nobody was able to explain exactly what had occurred.

According to the document, it seems the Royal Museum of Scotland had only recently taken delivery of a set canopic jars. These impressive clay pots each feature an animal head and are associated with the Four Sons of Horus, traditionally the guardians of the internal organs of the deceased.

As it transpired, a young Egyptologist had been officially assigned to look after the collection and, in an age when security was vastly more lax than it is now, must have decided to take one of these jars, a particularly fine specimen featuring a jackal's head, back to his lodgings in nearby Johnston Terrace.

What next occurred we shall never know. Suffice it to say that when the young man's absence was noticed a few days later, his lifeless, decaying corpse was found in his lodgings, spreadeagled over a chair. His hair had turned white and his eyes were bulging. Clutched tightly to his chest was the canopic jar with its lid removed.

His landlord, who made the discovery, promptly suffered a nervous breakdown. After a full police investigation, the post-mortem verdict attributed the young man's death to a heart attack. The jar featuring the jackal's head was discreetly returned to the museum, but the contents, whatever they might have been, had vanished.

A less terrifying, but more poignant story is told by the artist and cabaret impresario Andrew Brown who, when he purchased an apartment in Edinburgh's New Town, knew that the building had a substantial history. Adjoining the Royal Scots Club in Abercromby Place, the spacious first-floor rooms once formed part of the Royal Caledonian Club. Renovated and luxuriously restored, the property had for many years been occupied by Edinburgh's elite, but joining forces with the recently formed Royal Scots Club, shortly after the end of the First World War, served as a convalescent home for wounded soldiers.

Now, Andrew has survived a lifelong habit of entertaining friends into the small hours of the morning. His parties are always lively and eclectic and, after one such marathon, having finally dispersed his guests around 5 a.m., he awoke to find a bandaged male figure squatting on the floor beside his four-poster bed.

'I can't take this any more,' groaned the apparition and, rising unsteadily to his feet, staggered unsteadily over to an open window and threw himself out of it.

Although still barely awake, Andrew sprang from his bed and raced over to the by then closed window to see what had happened.

Peering out, he found everything in the garden below peaceful and undisturbed. 'There was no sign of a bandaged corpse anywhere to be seen,' he said in astonishment. 'When I explained what had happened to one of the staff at the Royal Scots Club, he told me that just such an incident had occurred back in 1918. The poor man was suffering from shell shock and had killed himself.'

But hauntings are not always associated with tragedies. Old rooms retain just as many happy memories as sad. Contented lives can have an equally powerful impact on their surroundings, and the majority of souls caught up in time-slips have led ordinary, unexceptional lives.

It was in 1970 that Christine Ross, who had moved to Edinburgh to work in graphic design, purchased a tenement flat in Comely Bank. 'It was completely empty when I moved in, but as soon as I walked through the front door I knew that it had been well cared for,' she recalled.

'The interiors were just as they must always have been, with the original cornice work and lovely old varnished comb work doors with brass handles. When I asked the lawyers, I discovered that it had previously belonged to a Mrs Duthie, who had lived there for all of her married life and had stayed on after her husband had died.

'Although we never met, I think Mrs Duthie must have been a very ordinary lady,' mused Chris. 'The feeling I had about the flat from the very beginning was that it had been occupied by a couple for several years, but that Mrs Duthie must have been on her own there for a long time afterwards. Everything was just as it should be.

'It seems very odd looking back on it now, but from the very start it never felt as if I was alone. I never saw anybody, but I could always feel a presence; a coolness. It didn't bother me much. In fact, I found it rather reassuring. Sometimes I'd move a piece of furniture, or knock something over, and I'd find myself saying, "Sorry, Mrs Duthie!"'

Christine did not mention anything about this to anyone. It was her own private joke. She had recently qualified in teacher training and started a job at Telford College. And as she had never before owned a home of her own, it proved very convenient when Alison, a friend and fellow teacher, rented a room from her.

'Alison lived there for a year and had a Norwegian boyfriend,' Christine said cheerfully. 'Before she moved out, she and her friend sat down and told me they knew they wouldn't have to worry about me because they knew there was somebody else living with me too!'

'You mean Mrs Duthie?' Christine had replied, and all three began to laugh.

That was the first indication she had been given that others were aware of Mrs Duthie. However, shortly after Alison moved out, Mary, a friend with two small sons, aged three and five, had asked if they could come to stay for a weekend. Mary's husband was varnishing the floors of their home and wanted them out of the way.

Christine naturally agreed, but, on the morning they were expected, Mary telephoned her to say that David, her five-year-old, had informed her that he was nervous about staying overnight because he knew that the flat was haunted. Nobody other than Alison and her Norwegian boyfriend had ever mentioned this before. Christine was amazed.

'It's all right, Mary, it's only Mrs Duthie,' Christine had reassured her friend.

This, of course, only made matters worse. 'I don't know what Mary must have thought of me, but I assured her I'd have a word with Mrs Duthie,' she said.

Naturally, she had no idea if this would work and to begin with she opened all of the doors and windows. She then informed Mrs Duthie in a loud voice that a small boy was coming to stay and would she mind going away for the weekend?

The family duly arrived and the next morning Christine asked David if he had felt the presence of a ghost? He said no.

'The sad thing was that after that Mrs Duthie never returned. I went on living in Comely Bank for another five years, but the atmosphere had changed,' said Christine. 'I really missed her.'

6

UNEXPECTED VISITORS

... there are many things which we are sure are true that you will not believe. What principle is there why the lodestone attracts iron? Why an egg produces a chicken by heat? Why a tree grows upwards, when the natural tendency of all things is downwards?

Dr Samuel Johnson, quoted in Boswell,
*The Journal of a Tour to the Hebrides
with Samuel Johnson, LL.D* (1786)

A full account of Jacqueline Heriot's ghostly experiences in Ceres is given in Chapter Four, but when I had originally arranged to meet up with her back in 2008, it was in connection with St Andrews Castle, where she was employed as a tour guide.

Only by going to St Andrews can you fully appreciate the dramatic setting and scale of this extraordinary, now ruined, fortification, and its adjoining cathedral, once the largest centre of Christian worship in Scotland.

The remains of the ancient castle squat defiantly on a steep clifftop overlooking the North Sea. More or less abandoned to become a ruin by the seventeenth century, the essential visitor attractions today are the notorious bottle dungeon, the cells and the kitchen tower.

The other features are the mine and counter-mine. These were created at the time of the castle siege, when the Earl of Arran, Governor of Scotland during the infancy of Mary Queen of Scots, attempted to evict its Protestant defenders while a fleet of offshore French galley ships pounded the battlements with canon. Step back for a moment and try to imagine what it must have been like for those who held the castle during that relentless onslaught.

Given her sensitivity at Ceres, Jacqueline Heriot might have expected to find herself under intense supernatural pressure, but says she has only once seen a ghost at the castle.

'We were closing up early,' she said. 'I was following my normal route, and had gone through the little gate from the Visitor Centre and onto the esplanade when I saw somebody leaning against the door of a cell on my left-hand side. Assuming it to be a late-comer, I took my time in approaching him but when I arrived at the doorway, there was nobody there.

'At first I thought he must have gone into the bottle dungeon but when I turned to look, it was empty. You know what it's like when your mind is on other things? I simply took it for granted there was somebody there and I can most certainly remember exactly what he looked like – he had long hair and wore a grey coat and trousers with long boots.

'I also remember him holding what looked like a bunch of keys. If he was neither a tourist nor a member of staff, it must have been a ghost like James Macpherson at Ceres, although I never actually saw him, only felt his presence. Perhaps the man I saw at the cell door was a jailer, or even a prisoner. He certainly didn't give the impression he'd noticed me.'

I have to admit that after the saga of James Macpherson, I found Jacqueline's revelation in St Andrews Castle a trifle lacking in originality, but then I was introduced to Monika Delinert, a castle guide since 2000.

Monika had been taking a friend from Austria to see the siege tunnel when she says she most definitely felt a hand grasping her shoulder and pulling her backwards.

'I thought it must have been my friend and turned to find out what she wanted. She was at least two metres behind me, so it couldn't have been her hand on my shoulder!'

It was hardly a life-defining moment, but it bothered Monika nonetheless. For weeks afterwards, she would find herself glancing nervously behind her whenever she took parties into the siege tunnel. Not necessarily of a nervous disposition, she was beginning to question her own sanity when one of the leaders of a school tour mentioned in passing that his father had installed the original lighting in the tunnel during the 1950s.

It had been a traumatic experience, she was told. The electrician had been going about his business as usual when he too had felt a cold hand on his shoulder, causing him to fall over backwards. When he had called out in alarm, he had realised that there was nobody else there. It had terrified him to the extent that he refused ever to set foot in that passageway again.

Although I'm not particularly brave, my own reaction under such circumstances, I suspect, would have been one of curiosity rather than fear. It's easy to say, but I don't think that anybody should be unsettled by signals from the past. They happen all the time.

Alison Campbell, a former producer with BBC Scotland, remembers her grandmother Janetta, known in the family as 'Nannie Campbell', telling her of a disconcerting incident during the 1940s. Nannie's husband, the Rev. George Campbell, was Minister of Kinclaven Parish Church, set in the pretty Perthshire countryside beside the River Tay, and they lived in the adjacent manse, with the kirkyard lying in between.

'There was no electricity in those days – the manse was lit by paraffin lamps,' explained Alison. 'Nannie Campbell played the organ for the Sunday services, and members of the church choir used to come to the manse on a weekday evening for choir practice. One November evening, as the choir were due to arrive, she realised she'd forgotten to bring over their hymn books from the church. Taking a small torch – this was deep in the countryside, remember; there were no street lights – she slipped out of the manse and into the blackness of a moonless night.'

The hinges of the War Memorial gateway into the kirkyard may have creaked as she passed under the stone arch, but otherwise all was silent. She heard no noise as she followed the yellow circle cast by her torch and strode briskly up to the kirk and opened the door.

'As she put it to me,' Alison said, '"And then I stepped back with a start, because it seemed to her that the church was full of people! Not only that, but they all seemed to be wearing old-fashioned clothes from another time entirely."'

'Nannie Campbell had a moment of panic,' continued Alison, 'but then gave herself a shake and told herself not to be silly; that if all these people were in church, they must be well-intentioned folk. Having reassured hereself, she walked down the aisle between the pews to the far end of the aisle, picked up an armful of hymn books from beside the organ and walked back again to the front entrance.

'And all of the time she felt herself being watched by this congregation. She let herself out of the door, walked back across the kirkyard and got on with the choir practice.'

Nannie Campbell was unable to explain it, except that perhaps she had been sensitive enough to 'tune in' to a service from bygone days. 'She was very definite that it was a real experience,' said Alison.

Whatever touches us, whatever appears to us, does so because whatever it is, or whatever it was, was once physically there. Think of it in terms of a hologram; everyday incidents caught in time and in general not in the least way threatening. Instead, we should count ourselves lucky to be chosen. And especially if there is more than one of you involved. Despite the popularity of ghost tours, the odds of manifestations being experienced at the same time by more than one person are, I am assured, rare.

It was a Sunday afternoon, and the German cabaret producer Lutz Deisinger and I were returning to Edinburgh by car, having had lunch with a friend in the small village of Dull, west of and above Aberfeldy. It was the first time Lutz had been to central Scotland and, as we were navigating the twisty road towards Weem, he caught sight of the bulk of Castle Menzies rising against its backdrop of wooded hills.

'What's that?' he asked.

'Castle Menzies,' I replied. 'It belonged to a Highland clan for 400 years. Bonnie Prince Charlie stayed there for two nights on his way north to fight at the Battle of Culloden in 1746.'

By this stage we had pulled up in front of the entrance driveway and could see that it was open to the public. 'Let's have a look,' he suggested.

The car park was completely empty and when we arrived in the front hall, the lady seated at a small kiosk table covered with souvenirs looked flustered. 'We're closing in twenty minutes,' she told us, glancing at her watch. 'Opening hours are between two and five o'clock, but you can have a quick look around if you wish.'

Despite her distracted welcome, she seemed pleased to see us. 'It's been very quiet today,' she confided.

The interiors of Castle Menzies could never be described as opulent, but the rugged thickness of the walls is impressive, and there is a dusty, lived in long ago atmosphere about the rooms. Restored and managed by the Clan Menzies Society, it survives as a typical example of a Highland stronghold that has seen better times.

After inspecting the old kitchen, we made a quick tour of the upper rooms. In one of them was a four-poster bed covered with a beautiful antique blanket. On the first floor we found a long drawing room hung with portraits of various Menzies chiefs. As we were inspecting the paintings, two women and a small child joined us. As they passed, one of the women turned and smiled, but said nothing. The child ran ahead excitedly. All three of them appeared to be relaxed and happy.

Time rushed past and since it was almost five o'clock, Lutz and I descended the stairway to the front hall, where the lady behind the table was preoccupied with tidying up. After selling us a couple of postcards, she said, 'That's good, I can close up now.'

'Don't forget the people upstairs,' said Lutz.

'What people upstairs?' She seemed surprised.

I explained that we had passed two women and a child in the drawing room, and she looked worried. 'But there's been nobody else here today,' she protested.

'Yes there are,' I said. 'They were on the floor above when we last saw them.'

Lutz nodded in confirmation, and she left the desk to go upstairs and see for herself. We could hear her footsteps clattering around on the floorboards above, and shortly afterwards she reappeared. 'There's definitely nobody else here,' she announced crossly, adding, 'You had me worried for a moment.'

Lutz and I looked at each other in amazement. 'Come on,' he said. 'It's not our problem.'

Outside, our car was the only vehicle in the car park. It had started to drizzle, so we headed towards the A9 at speed.

7

THE PEOPLE UPSTAIRS

For many lang year I hae heard frae my grannie
Of brownies an' bogles by yon castle wa',
Of auld withered hags that were never thought cannie,
An' fairies that danced till they heard the cock craw.

Richard Gall, 'The Hazlewood Witch' (*c.* 1800)

It is now over twenty years since the writer and sportsman Maxwell Macleod purchased a seventeenth-century mill conversion on the banks of the River Almond in Midlothian. At the time he was employed as a freelance journalist, writing articles for a string of newspapers, and had become perfectly accustomed to working late into the night. 'I was concentrating on a news story,' he recalled. 'I had drunk no alcohol, and the only "flaky" thing going on was that I was nearing a deadline and working at full pitch, so therefore slightly jumpy. I'd also been drinking copious cups of coffee and needed to answer the call of nature.'

Answering the call required Maxwell to go upstairs to a bathroom where, as he was about to step through the door, he found a strange woman standing beside the radiator, no more than a pace away from him. 'She was at right-angles to me and wearing a grey dress of a cheap kind, with a grey lace apron and white shawl,' he said. 'The shawl seemed to be integrated into her bonnet, which she was holding in place with her left hand. Her right hand was at her side.

'She had a long nose,' he added. 'I couldn't see her eyes, but I got the impression she was agitated by my company. This was no misty might-have-been hallucination. She was standing under a bare light bulb as clear as day.

'Height? No more than five foot one, and she seemed to be standing on something a little below floor level. There was a certain shakiness about her. Her age? She was perhaps in her early sixties, not much older.'

Unperturbed, Maxwell stood his ground and called out softly to his resident housekeeper, who was in her room downstairs. 'Anna, come here now!'

There was no response from below, so he shouted out more loudly, 'Anna, come here NOW!'

Anna shouted back that she had gone to bed, but Maxwell persisted. 'ANNA!' At this point, the apparition vanished into thin air.

'As you know, I'm not the sort of person who sees ghosts,' asserted Maxwell indignantly. 'I was working full time as a news-paper reporter at the time. I knew about writing what I saw, no more, no less. I don't make things up.'

But as anyone in journalism will tell you, professional news-paper reporters always check out their stories before going into print. On further investigation, therefore, Maxwell discovered that he was far from being alone in having encountered the lady in the cap and apron. It soon emerged that she was something of a local celebrity.

'Long before the mill was transformed into a dwelling house, it incorporated a shop,' he explained. 'The lady I'd seen was the shopkeeper. Dozens of people around here have run into her.'

That may well be true, but Maxwell admits he has not had the privilege of seeing her since that first encounter. Perhaps he gave her too much of a shock.

Hauntings, whether we believe in them or not, are rarely life-threatening and it never fails to puzzle me when people speak of being terrified by a ghost. Why should they be? With the exception of poltergeists and perhaps a handful of comic-strip demons, lost souls are rarely out to get us. We have nothing to be afraid of unless our conscience tells us otherwise.

Nor should we expect the spirits of the past to perform to order. It exasperates me when I hear of friends who have deliberately set out on a ghost hunt and been disappointed when nothing occurred. It just does not work like that.

Admittedly, there are places and situations where the likelihood of the past overlapping with the present is more probable – period homes filled with the passing of generations; settings of cruelty, violence and despair. The love and the hate generated within such walls can be overwhelming. But you cannot expect to buy tickets. At least not for the unexpected.

The Citizens Theatre in the Gorbals of Glasgow is a location resonating in end-of-an-era charm, and you can actually feel it: the anxiety behind stage; the excitement of the curtain rising; the applause of an opening night, and the murmur of the audience as it disperses when the curtain falls. But this is show business and what would you expect otherwise?

Dating from 1878 but renamed the Citizens Theatre with an egalitarian flourish in 1945, the theatre's commitment to low-priced tickets has made it one of the most innovative stages in Europe. As a regular supporter during the 1980s, I marvelled at the intimate arena with its sloped seating levels, thinking it hard to find anywhere more compelling for the ghosts of the stage to linger. But then again, it does not work like that.

Working first with Philip Prowse, then the equally brilliant Robert David MacDonald, Giles Havergal was director of the Citizens Theatre from 1969 until 2003, and is adamant that he never encountered anything of a supernatural nature over that period. 'I always found the interiors far too benign and welcoming to be haunted,' he says, which coming from such a perspicacious individual was not what I had expected to hear.

However, it does confirm that not everybody is susceptible to the twilight world. Irrespective of creativity, there are those who are infinitely more receptive to shadows than others and in theatrical circles, the Citizens is famous for its rarely glimpsed occupants.

A typical anecdote, for example, concerned a long-serving member of staff who, finding herself trapped in the Upper Circle during a power cut, was led to safety below by a silent figure wearing a monk's habit. At first she had assumed he was a member of the cast, but afterwards found that no such character existed in the play being performed that night.

Audiences seated in the Dress Circle during the 1970s were often intrigued by the costumed 'actor' who sat boldly on the balcony and glared at them while ignoring what was taking place on stage. More recent members of staff have commented on the lady in the Victorian gown who glides elegantly from the Dress Circle Bar towards the Circle Studio dressing rooms. A security guard on his late-night rounds 'distinctly felt the swish of her dress as she overtook him in the Props and Costume Department'.

Far be it for me to imply that such sightings are mere flights of fancy, although you might expect there to be mind games under circumstances where emotions have run high through the passage of time. For example, in religious seminaries and retreats where the devout congregate for seclusion and prayer.

One such retreat is the Cistercian Abbey of Nunraw in East Lothian. Founded as a nunnery, it remained in private owner-ship for the best part of four centuries before being reclaimed by the Cistercian brotherhood from Ireland in 1945. Since then the old red-stone visitor centre and the spacious, airy cloisters built by the monks themselves, have provided a haven of peace and tranquillity for anyone in search of spiritual solitude.

Nobody asks questions and there is always a bed for the night on the basis that visitors make a contribution in proportion to what they can afford. In addition, the monks are kindly and non-judgemental, and always at hand to listen. It was therefore to Nunraw that Elizabeth Davies escaped when her marriage ran into trouble, and she has been a devotee of the monastery ever since. However, to this day she can vividly recall the first night she stayed over in the guest dormitory.

'It was mid-winter, and we were three ladies, myself and Ruth and Jane, and one man, whose name I can't remember,' she explained. 'For some time we all sat with Father Benedict drink-ing coffee in front of the fire before retiring to our rooms, the man to the men's dormitory, and Ruth, myself and Jane to ours.

'There were three of us occupying the bedroom, and we all woke up simultaneously,' she continued. 'My bed was beside the door, and although I was still half asleep, I could hear Jane's voice saying anxiously, "There's somebody in the room. He's beside you."'

Elizabeth had looked up to find a luminous figure wearing what appeared to be an old duffel coat looming over her. What was even more alarming was that she could clearly see the bed-room door and door knob glowing on the far side of him, as if he were transparent.

'I began to say my prayers,' she said with a shudder as the memory returned to her. 'But I kept one eye open, and as I recited the words out loud, the vision faded back through the open door and I could see a shadow walking up the stairs towards the men's room. We all looked at each other in amazement. We'd all of us seen the same thing, so nobody could have accused me of making it up.'

Detractors sometimes dismiss such phenomena as the natural aberration of our sensory powers, but is this a good enough reason to do so? Aristotle famously observed that human beings share five common senses – sight, hearing, touch, taste and smell. We also know that beyond these lie instincts such as self-awareness, which create all kinds of unanswered questions. Why, for example, does the hair on the back of a neck involuntarily tingle in response to a poignant tune or an emotional lift? How is it possible for amputees to feel phantom pain in limbs which are no longer there?

Science has a long way to go before it arrives at an honest and uncompromising understanding of the supernatural. And in the meantime we can only rationalise what we can.

Scholars have argued the causes of good and evil since time immemorial. There are loads of logical explanations, but nothing is ever that simple. Wickedness leaves its scars not only on its victims but on its perpetrators. When bad things happen, repercussions follow.

On a lonely stretch of the Dumbarton Road in Dunbartonshire an encounter with the Black Lady of Dalquhurn brings immediate death to anyone unfortunate enough to be in the wrong place at the wrong time. Of course, you might well ask how anyone knows about this if no one has lived to tell the tale?

Well, it seems a John Neil from Renton did live to tell the tale, and spilled the beans in his last breath. However, the mystery becomes even more obscure when it emerges that the Black Lady of Dalquhurn is, in all probability, not a lady at all, but a man.

Up until 1989, the so-called 'Tomb of the Black Lady' sat just inside a gateway to the railway siding of the former Dalquhurn Bleach Works, fifty yards from the River Leven. How or when it came to be identified with the Black Lady is unknown, but clues to the ownership can be taken from the tombstone inscription which was recorded in the *Country Reporter* of 10 December 1969:

HIC SITUS EST
GEORGIUS SCOTT
AUDENTO FILIUS
MERCATORI
NUPER GLASGUENSIS
ANNOS QUINDECIM
IN INDIA COMMEMORATI
STATIM POST REDIITI
IN BRITTANNIUM
LONDON OBIIT:
SEXTO DIES NOVEMBRI
ANN: MDCCLXVII
AETATIS SUA XXXVII
RELIQUIAS EIUS ILLINC
(FR)ATRIBUS CAROLO ET
GULIELMI
(LATA). HIC CONDI VOLLUIT.

(Note: letters in brackets were found to be illegible.)

Translated, this reads: 'Here is buried George Scott, son of a gallant merchant, late of Glasgow. He lived for fifteen years in India, and died immediately on his return to London, Great Britain, on

6 November 1787. His age was 37 years. His remains brought by his brothers Charles and William from latter place (London?), he wished to be preserved here.'

Local historian Graham Hopner has meticulously researched the subject and has reached the conclusion that George Scott was one of three brothers – George, William and Charles – all of them born at Dalquhurn Cottage. Their parents were Lawrence and Margaret Scott, and Charles, having accumulated a small fortune from the bleachworks, purchased Dalquhurn House from the Telfer Smollett family in either 1774 or 1775.

In 1969, an article featured in the *Country Reporter* led four anglers on the River Leven to claim that at the end of a night's fishing they had been touched by a weird and ethereal white form which afterwards had vanished in the direction of Dalquhurn. Soon afterwards, another correspondent wrote in to say that his wife had seen a mystical figure resembling a woman, standing upriver from George Scott's tomb. Other reports soon followed, all involving a woman in black.

The legend of the Black Lady has been circulating around the Renton district for well over 200 years. But who was she, this Black Lady? And what connection did she have to the final resting place of George Scott?

One possibility is that the Dalquhurn tomb, which measures sixteen feet square, might contain more than one occupant. There is the suggestion that Scott might have returned from India with a companion, a lady friend or even an ayah with whom he had formed a relationship.

Such speculation, however, was discounted when it was confirmed that only one body was interred in the Scott mausoleum. So was George Scott perchance a transvestite? Or was it simply that he wore his hair long, in the fashion of the eighteenth century?

In 1991, a Balloch businessman, having purchased the site of the Dalquhurn Bleach Works for redevelopment, applied for permission to remove the tomb. Nobody can confirm for certain what then took place, but following a prolonged correspondence with the local authority, it seems that George's grave was desecrated and his skeleton deposited a few miles away, in the Alexandria Cemetery.

When word of this got out there was outrage among the local community, especially when some Renton schoolchildren were found playing with human bones. By this stage, an impasse had been reached between the businessman and the council, and what made matters worse was a ruling that since the tomb was on private, not public, land, there were no legal requirements for it to be maintained irrespective of the last wishes of its occupant.

Since then, the site of the tomb of the Black Lady has remained untouched, which is not so surprising when you consider that generations of Renton weans have been told that if they do not behave, the Black Lady of Dalquhurn will get them. Meanwhile, the grisly relics of George Scott are being stored in Alexandria. Is it any wonder that the Black Lady of Dalquhurn, whoever she or he might be, walks the Dumbarton Road at night looking for the despoilers of his or her last resting place?

The advice I would therefore offer to anyone finding themselves on the Renton stretch of the Dumbarton Road after sunset is simply to maintain a healthy stride. When driving a car, be certain to keep your eyes firmly fixed on the highway ahead.

Under absolutely no circumstances should you feel tempted to pull over and offer someone a lift.

8

TO TRIUMPH IN GLORY
WITH THE LAMB

When a man's soul is certainly in hell, his body will
scarce lie quiet in a tomb, however costly; some time
or other the door must open, and the reprobate come
forth in the abhorred garments of the grave.

Robert Louis Stevenson,
Edinburgh: Picturesque Notes (1879)

The religious purges of long ago are of little concern to those facing
up to the challenges of the here and now. There are, nonetheless,
certain episodes of repression indelibly imprinted on the faiths of
our island race, their consequences embedded deep within our
spiritual psyche. That is why we shudder when we hear of atroci-
ties in far-off lands. That is why we claim to abhor injustice.

The Scottish National Covenant of 400 years ago is a case
in point. The passions it engendered are largely forgotten, but
they certainly make it easier to explain the re-emergence of such
movements as Islamic Fundamentalism.

In 1633, spurred on by William Laud, the Anglican Archbishop
of Canterbury, King Charles I, a didactic monarch by any

standards, pronounced himself head of the Church of Scotland by Divine Right and, in so doing, ordered the replacement of the reformer John Knox's *Book of Discipline* with his own modified *Book of Common Prayer.* This was seen by the majority of Lowland Scots as a betrayal of everything that had come before.

Since neither the Scottish Parliament nor the Kirk Assembly had been consulted, the king's proposals were justifiably seen as a blatant attempt to undermine the independence of Scotland's hard-won fight for its Presbyterian faith. Although the majority of Scots had always supported their Stuart monarchs in the past, this was a step too far. Matters came to a head on 23 July 1637 when Jenny Geddes, a market trader in Edinburgh, threw her 'fald' stool at the minister of St Giles' Kirk in protest. When, in 1638, a large number of devout members of the Church of Scotland signed a National Covenant of opposition, it ignited a period of brutal religious repression which lasted for over fifty years.

During these 'killing times', simple, God-fearing folk, whose only crime was to reject the corruption of their political masters, were unwittingly transformed into martyrs. Those who failed to attend government-approved churches were fined. The death penalty was imposed on those who preached out-of-doors at so-called 'conventicles'.

It is estimated that over 28,000 souls met their deaths in the violent confrontations that followed. With such an intensity of anger and frustration, it is only to be expected that the blanket of discontent surrounding such emotions should linger on to create the occasional aberration of time.

Encroaching upon Edinburgh to the south-west are the Pentland Hills, today designated a Regional Park. Here the scenery is criss-crossed by rivulets, burns and glens spilling into the Southern Uplands, a wild and lonely territory despite its close proximity to Edinburgh.

And it was exactly the plentiful solitude and fresh air to be found here that attracted the Dutton family. Entrapped within their individual working environments during the week, Richard Dutton, a bank employee, and his wife Emma, a nurse, first began excursions prior to their marriage. With the arrival of their two sons, Jamie and Pete, such outings became a monthly ritual in all weathers.

More often than not, they parked their car in the old railway station at Dolphinton, and set off on foot towards West Linton. They had completed this walk on numerous occasions, but one Sunday, as they were crossing the gate at North Slipperfield, the sky became rapidly overcast and before long it had begun to rain.

'It'll pass,' said Richard. Besides, all four were equipped with boots and waterproofs.

Two miles on, as they were approaching the remains of the old Blackhill farmhouse, they encountered a man dressed in what looked like an ill-fitting coat. He was carrying what appeared to be a younger man over his shoulder. 'Can we help?' asked Richard. 'My wife is a nurse.'

The older man fixed them with a sad and vacant stare, and made no response. Turning to Emma and the boys, Richard shrugged his shoulders. 'Must be down-and-outs,' he observed. 'Probably drunk.'

Emma was not so censorious. 'The one wearing the red cloak looked unconscious,' she said with concern. When they turned to have another look, the pair had vanished.

'They went over the brow of that hill,' shouted Jamie, scampering across the heather with his brother to have a look. 'Not here,' he called back to his parents. 'They must have gone some other way.'

Sure enough, when Richard and Emma reached the summit, the strange couple were nowhere to be seen.

'Did you see how they were dressed?' asked Emma. 'They must belong to one of those historical reenactment groups. You know, the Sealed Knot or White Cockade Society.'

Richard laughed. 'Well at least I'll have something to tell them in the office tomorrow.'

Emma was more circumspect. 'I've a bad feeling about this,' she said and, as soon as they reached home and the children were fed, she turned on the computer to search the internet. 'Look what it says here,' she called out eventually. Richard joined her and, with some incredulity, absorbed the information on the screen.

On 28 November 1666, a bloody battle was fought at Rullion Green on the southern slopes of the Pentland Hills. Some 900 Covenanters, men and boys, had been challenged by a Government army led by the notorious General 'Black' Tam Dalyell. It was a rout. Fifty Covenanters were killed outright. The remainder scattered into the surrounding hillsides.

Although badly wounded, young John Carphin, an Ayrshire lad, was among those who escaped, but by midnight his strength had failed him. He therefore sought help at the remote farmhouse of Blackhill where Adam Sanderson, a shepherd, invited him in. Knowing that this would place Sanderson in danger, Carphin declined and asked only that he help him make his way up the valley of the West Water.

Sanderson obliged, leading him in the right direction, but as dawn broke the younger man collapsed and died in his arms, his last words a plea to be buried within sight of his beloved Ayrshire hills. It was a big favour to ask of a complete stranger, especially as it put his companion at considerable personal risk should his actions become known. However, Adam Sanderson was a decent man, unimpressed by religious bigotry.

So he carried the body of John Carphin to the summit of the Black Law, where the far-off Ayrshire hills could clearly be seen in the far distance. There he buried him and erected a cairn of stones in his memory.

'It doesn't seem possible, but I wonder?' speculated Emma.

A few weeks later, she and Richard, Jamie and Pete made a return visit to Blackhill. This time they climbed to the top of Black Law, where a gravestone erected two centuries after the interment marks the spot of John Carphin's final resting place. By the time the gravestone was erected the covenanting cause had long been resolved, but its martyrs are not forgotten.

The day was bright and clear. To the west, through the gap between Black Law and the Pike, the Dutton family could clearly make out the distant, silken hills of Ayrshire. 'He'd have liked that,' said Emma with a sigh.

Another chapter in the turbulent advance of Scotland's story concerns the relentless thieving of cattle the length of the 'Debatable Land', the Border with England. From the thirteenth until seventeenth centuries, the practice was commonplace, becoming a way of life for the lawless 'riding' clans who dominated this territory and regularly turned against each other in their struggle to survive. As a result, the Borders region is littered with medieval keeps and peel towers, each and every one of them with blood on its stones. As darkness falls, who knows whose eyes are keeping watch on their cold stone battlements?

On the summit of Minto Crags, near Denholm, are the remains of Fatlips Castle, so named to commemorate the swollen jowls and mouth of the notorious Turnbull of Barnhill, who never passed up a chance to kiss a pretty girl. Standing three storeys high and towering above the surrounding countryside, this formidable stronghold occupies a spectacular vantage point. From its clifftop platform, known as Barnhill's Bed, approaching trouble was easily spotted and, in the relentless days of reiving and English invasion, this proved invaluable.

The crunch for the Turnbulls came in the early sixteenth century, when King James IV, despairing of the lawlessness of his Border subjects, held a mass hanging beside the Rule Water, two miles from Denholm. Fatlips Castle passed to their neighbours and rivals, the Elliotts, who were elevated to the Scottish peerage as earls of Minto.

From then on, the fortified tower on the hill became little more than a garden folly for the Elliotts until 1897, when it was restored as a sporting lodge. It then became a museum, but after a spate of vandalism which culminated in a fire, it was abandoned.

That was back in the 1970s, and since then those who live nearby in the area have looked on in dismay as the building has deteriorated. 'I often go for a wee walk up there on a weekend,' Sandy Lochie informed me, 'But never at night.'

Although he and his friends played as children in and around the tower, he claims to be baffled as to why it was abandoned by its owners. 'It's perfectly habitable,' he insists, and, to some extent, this is what prompted him to stop one night as he was driving past and noticed lights flickering in the windows.

'There was only just a dull glow, but I knew there shouldn't have been anybody up there,' he recalled.

Besides, he knew that access from ground level had been bricked up. 'I had three options,' he went on. 'I could have gone home and forgotten about it, or I could have reported it to the police, or, instead, I could go and have a look for myself – which is what I did.'

Pulling his car into the side of the road, Sandy extracted a torch from the car's glove compartment and cautiously made his way up the overgrown track. 'I must have been daft,' he said. 'But it was a warmish night and I didn't really think much of it at the time.'

As he came closer to the castle walls, he says he clearly heard the sounds of a harp or clarsach being played. 'There was a great roar of shouting, joviality and laughter, as if the occupants were throwing a party.'

By then he was within twenty feet of the castle walls. Increasingly breathless from the ascent, he had momentarily paused when a loud explosion rocked the ground and everything became quiet. Looking up, he saw the lights in the tower windows had been turned off.

'There was a pungent smell of damp smoke, even though it hadn't rained all week,' he recalled with a shudder. 'Everything was eerily still. I said to myself "you're a daft laddie", and turned on my heels to go home.'

Sandy returned the following morning to have another look at the castle by daylight. As he might have expected, he found the entrance was sealed up and there were no apparent signs of a break-in.

'I took the dog along with me this time,' he said. 'Poor old chap, he started off by running away ahead of me, but as we got closer he stopped dead in his tracks and started to whimper.

'From there on, he wouldn't go any further. I reckon he knew something was going on there. If only animals could speak.'

9

HELL AND PURGATORY

Strange things, the neighbours say, have happen'd here;
Wild shrieks have issued from the hollow tombs;
Dead men have come again, and walk'd about;
And the great bell has toll'd, unrung, untouch'd.

The Reverend Robert Blair, 'The Grave' (1743)

Nowhere is the past more pervasive than on the Orkney Islands, where everyday survival is governed by 100-mile-per-hour winds off the Atlantic Ocean. In one of his more memorable essays published in the *Orkney Herald*, the Orcadian poet George Mackay Brown recalled a childhood visit to two adjoining crofts named Hell and Purgatory. Around thirty years ago I noticed an advertisement offering these two crofts with their six acres of land for sale for what appeared to be an extremely modest sum. At the time I thought how splendid it would be to have such an address on my headed notepaper.

But then I asked myself why they were so named? And why so inexpensive?

So I consulted a map and immediately saw the reason. Perched on the very edge of the far north-east coast and no doubt glorious during the warm summer months, during winter they are exposed to everything the North Atlantic chooses to throw at them. Hell and Purgatory, indeed!

Such weather conditions are at the core of a thousand Orcadian and Shetland folktales, where the spirits of all of the forces of land, sea and sky become one. Added to which, there is no more evocative a stretch of water, where the rain clouds thicken, and the ocean clamours for attention, than Scapa Flow. Even on a fair day with a light head wind, the mood remains solemn; the great mass of water looms in front of you like a solemn sheet of steel.

Here, seventy-four ships of the German High Seas fleet were deliberately scuttled by their crews in the last century. Moreover, on a chill October night in 1939, 833 seamen lost their lives when a German U-Boat torpedoed the HMS *Royal Oak*, a battleship employed as temporary accommodation for sailors.

In 2006, Rick Moston and Gus Purdy, both experienced scuba divers, arrived in Stromness to join a team of naval history enthusiasts exploring the basin of Scapa Flow. On 21 June 1919, Admiral von Reuter, the German commander, had issued the order for his entire fleet to be sunk. Although many of the boats have since been salvaged, the bottom of the sea is still littered with remnants: three 25,000-ton battleships, four cruisers, five torpedo boats and two submarines, not to mention a handful of other more domestic wrecks.

Rick and Gus had been on similar excursions before, but never one with such sinister associations. Only too well did Gus remember his grandfather reminiscing about a friend who had gone down on the *Royal Oak*. Today, it lies in a protected war grave, keeping company with HMS *Vanguard*, another battleship which was blown up in 1917, condemning her crew to a watery tomb. Diving in this vicinity is strictly forbidden, but elsewhere in Scapa Flow it has been actively encouraged.

Starting off with the big ships, SMS *König* and SMS *Kronprinz Wilhelm*, Rick and Gus moved on to SMS *Köln* and SMS *Dresden*, taking time off to swim with some seals off the so-called Barrel of Butter.

It was on the fourth day of their adventure that Gus dived close to where the SMS *Karlsruhe* lay, surrounded by debris. Reaching the bottom, he was preoccupied with the scallops, queenies, plume anemones and dead men's fingers clinging to its sides, when his attention was diverted to a similar vessel lying on its starboard side.

'I'd started to encircle the hull, when I noticed a yellow light coming from inside one of the portholes on the bridge. I thought it was odd and when I paused beside it to have a look, I saw this bloated face of a middle-aged man staring back at me.'

Gus shuddered. 'I can't tell you what a shock it gave me. I'll never forget those watery eyes. He didn't have a mask on or a wet suit, which naturally alarmed me. Then I realised he was trying to say something to me.

'His situation looked desperate. All of the time, he was scrabbling frantically at the porthole surrounds with his hands. The water was swirling all over him. He looked absolutely terrified.'

Unnerved, Gus broke surface to summon help and was quickly joined by Rick. 'When we dived, I tried to locate the sunken boat, but it was no longer there,' said Gus incredulously. 'Rick thought I was winding him up. He didn't think it at all funny. But I wouldn't have made something like that up,' he told me afterwards. 'I'm not that sick. It was far too dreadful to be a joke, a really bad dream. It still haunts me. I just hope I was having a bad turn and that there isn't somebody still down there.'

There are a few places on earth where there is a real sense of being where time began, and the Orkney Islands rank high in this category. Remote as they might seem to some of us, a lasting impression has been left by the two World Wars. Gus Purdy is unlikely ever to forget his diving exploit in Scapa Flow, but even more recently yet another equally disturbing experience was shared by two young Norwegians on a walking holiday.

Off the west coast of Mainland at eight o'clock in the evening of 5 June 1916, the HMS *Hampshire* on its way to Russia was sunk by either a mine or a German torpedo. Now, most of us still recognise the famous moustache and pointing figure of the First World War's most iconic recruitment poster. Herbert Kitchener, Earl Kitchener of Khartoum, was the British Government's Secretary of State for War, but how many of us know that he was on board HMS *Hampshire* on the fateful night it disappeared under the waves?

Conspiracy theories abound. To this day nobody can be certain if it was a German mine or torpedo, or an internal explosion that was responsible. Watching from Marwick Head, Joe Angus, a gunner with the Orkney Territorial Forces, reported seeing the ship on fire two miles offshore. Within fifteen minutes it had disappeared from sight. There were 200 survivors who clung to rafts and pieces of wreckage in the raging sea, but 656 perished, including the Secretary of State for War.

Only twelve members of the crew made land, and it was reported that Lord Kitchener had last been seen on the quarter-deck. His mission to Russia was top secret, but it was later revealed that he was carrying a number of critically important official documents. When the sinking was confirmed, the Admiralty hastily ordered precautions to prevent any wreckage falling into enemy hands.

Lord Kitchener's body was never found. A recommended read on the subject is Donald McCormick's *The Mystery of Lord Kitchener's Death* published in 1958, but the contents of this fascinating book have little to do with what took place when

What the future holds in store for all of us. Greyfriars Kirkyard, Edinburgh, site of the Covenanters' graveyard

Ewan Irvine (centre) and the team of Edinburgh GhostFest 2008

The Camera Obscura and The Ragged School, Edinburgh

A child's pram in the Ragged School

Bill Caffray at Inverchaolain, 2008

Knockdow House, Cowal

TOP. St Andrews Castle

MIDDLE. Johnston Terrace, Edinburgh, haunt of the Cynocephalus

RIGHT. Mary Crawshay, The Green Lady of Torosay on Mull (photo courtesy of Christopher James)

TOP. Castle Menzies, Weem, Perthshire

MIDDLE. Aleister Crowley

BOTTOM. The Sleeping Beauty mountain, Isle of Lewis

ABOVE. Edinburgh's Cowgate, which burst into flames on the night of 7 December 2002

RIGHT. The Witches' Fountain, Edinburgh Castle

The gravel sweep of Fingask Castle (photo courtesy of Andrew Murray Threipland)

The ruins of St Martin's Kirk, Haddington

Ackergill Castle, Wick

my Scandinavian friends found themselves looking for accommodation in the coastal village of Birsay. Or do they?

Birgitta and Per, both keen bird-watchers, had flown across to Kirkwall from Oslo, and, while on an evening stroll on the cliffs beside the Brough Lighthouse, came across a small group of men who appeared lost. In their midst was a stout, medium height figure wrapped in a soiled trench coat.

'They all looked as if they were soaked to the skin,' said Per. 'Yet it hadn't been raining. In fact, it was a very pleasant evening. I thought that was very odd. Birgitta said they looked as if they had been in the sea, but under the circumstances it seemed very unlikely.'

'The man we spoke to was definitely confused,' added Birgitta. 'When I asked him if they needed help, he just turned away and walked off without saying a word.'

Nearby was a stone tower which Per and Birgitta were later informed was a memorial to a famous British soldier who had died in the First World War. When Per mentioned their experience to their landlady, she laughed out loud.

'That'll be himself,' she said. 'Lord Kitchener. You're not the first to have seen him.'

Neither Birgitta nor Per had any idea who Lord Kitchener was, but back in Norway Birgitta was busy Googling one night on the internet and, on a whim, typed in the name name, 'Lord Kitchener'.

'Come and look at this,' she called out to Per in excitement.

Staring from the computer screen was the man with the moustache they had met on the clifftops at Birsay.

10

FOR THOSE IN PERIL ON
THE SEA

They that go down to the sea in ships,
And occupy their business on the great waters;
These men see the works of the Lord,
and his wonders in the deep.

Book of Psalms
Psalm 106: 23–24

The sea is a hard taskmaster, and Scotland's ragged coastline, with its harbours, beaches, secret inlets and hidden coves, has known more than its fair share of misfortune. It is a cruel and uncompromising existence and they who live by its shores to earn a living from its depths are invariably possessed with a deal of stoicism which the rest of us can only marvel at.

The Cowal Peninsula lodges between the mouth of the Firth of Clyde and Loch Fyne in southern Argyll, a coastal landscape punctuated by opulent Victorian villas and yachting marinas. Despite the half-hour ferries ploughing backwards and forwards between Gourock and Dunoon, Cowal can often feel strangely detached from the rest of Scotland.

South of Dunoon, on Loch Striven, is Inverchaolain Lodge, a former shooting lodge on the Knockdow estate which I visited in Chapter One. Richly forested, this hidden corner of Scotland played an important role in meeting the desperate demand for timber during the First World War. Over this difficult period, Inverchaolain Lodge was requisitioned for the Women's Land Army Timber Corps and from 1941, some thirty or more patriotic young women were stationed here to fell trees and assist at the local sawmill.

And it was early in 1943 that one such recruit found herself returning from weekend leave a day early. Ordinarily, she would have stayed overnight in Dunoon, but despite knowing that she would be the first of her group to arrive, she decided instead to cycle the ten or more miles to the lodge.

The moon was rising as she set off, and its mellow light cast an eerie glow over the seascape. As she pedalled past Loch Striven, she heard the grey seals barking on the shoreline. Deep in the forest, the trees rustled and sighed. Small animals scurried into the undergrowth.

When she arrived, Inverchaolain Lodge was empty as she had expected. She briskly stored her bicycle in the shed and fetched the front-door key from its usual hiding place. Since the cook had not, as yet, returned, the lodge kitchen was chilly and bare, so she went straight to her bed. But as she lay warm beneath her blanket listening to the hush of the loch outside, she saw the bedroom door open and shut, and heard a soft swishing sound. 'It sounded like fabric sweeping across the floor,' she recalled.

Frozen stiff in her army cot, she could hear her heart pounding, all the more so when a dim, shadowy figure glided over to the window. It appeared to be a young woman, who stopped in front of the glass to gaze out towards the loch. She looked so sad and moaned unhappily before turning around to exit through the closed door.

Uncertain what to do next, the recruit lay mesmerised under her covers until she eventually found the courage to rally herself. With a Tilley lamp to light her way, she cautiously ventured downstairs into the hallway below and, glancing out of the window onto a moonlit lawn, saw an extraordinary sight.

Where the bicycle shed normally stood was a thatched cottage covered in roses. The garden too was full of lovely flowers. In front of the cottage door stood the same woman she had seen upstairs. Beside her was a young man wearing knee-breeches and a cut-away jacket.

He was kissing her goodbye and the girl was sobbing. As the young man turned to walk towards the loch, a small fishing boat appeared on the horizon. As it drew close to the shore, the loch turned suddenly wild and stormy, with huge waves dashing onto the shingle.

As the recruit watched in astonishment, she could see the girl striding backwards and forwards along the shoreline, wringing her hands in sorrow. Then suddenly both she and the cottage faded away and the shed reappeared as if from nowhere.

When the other trainees arrived the following morning, their colleague gave them a full account of what she had witnessed and was told that it served her right for spending a night at the lodge on her own. Loch Striven, she learned, was infamous for its sudden storms and unpredictable currents. Nobody has ever kept track of the number of boats that have been lost in this solemn and unpredictable stretch of water.

Such anecdotes, of course, are replicated from the Solway Firth to Cape Wrath, from John O' Groats to Dunbar, vivid accounts of fishing disasters, lost souls, piracy, brigandage and smuggling.

Before lighthouses were built, the deliberate wrecking of passing vessels was rife off the East Lothian coast. Cargoes of wine, brandy, wood, fruit, grain and coal regularly washed ashore, and it was the coastal dwellers' attitude towards plunder that prompted the author Robert Louis Stevenson to collaborate with his stepson Lloyd Osbourne in writing his last novel, *The Wrecker*, in 1892. Stevenson's childhood holidays were spent with relatives in North Berwick and Auldhame exploring the East Lothian coastline and he, more than anyone, understood how the past leaves its ever-present stamp on the future. Loss and the debris of human tragedy are timeless.

It was a summer's afternoon in 2007 when Avril Kirk, whom we will encounter again in Chapter Thirteen, set off to explore Skateraw Harbour, south of Dunbar, where she came across the ruins of some old cottages and on an impulse followed the pathway to Chapel Point, which has a raised beach.

Rank forces were at work that day. On Chapel Point, Avril found herself pausing in front of an old stone step. 'All of a sudden there was a loud booming noise,' she remembered.

'I was standing in front of a large wooden cross and all around me the light was dimming. There was a small church behind the cross and I could hear waves crashing and seagulls shrieking. On the pathway ahead of me I could see dark shapes carrying what looked like bodies up from the beach and into the church.'

In a flash, everything changed back to normal, and Avril stood where she was, stunned. 'When I arrived home I didn't want to tell anyone about what had happened in case they thought I'd lost my mind,' she said. 'It was very confusing.'

On a subsequent visit to Dunbar House Museum, however, all became clear. Quite by chance Avril found herself talking to a genealogist. It is always easier to confide in a stranger whom you are unlikely to see again and when she mentioned her visit to Skateraw, he confirmed that there had once been an ancient chapel dedicated to St Dennis on Chapel Point.

'It was there long before the cottages were built,' he told her. 'And the only thing left when it was demolished was a wooden cross which was later moved to the car park when a World War Two memorial to the Canongate Boys' Club was erected.'

When Avril shyly recounted what had happened to her, he seemed unaffected. 'Before the lighthouses were built, there were hundreds of ships wrecked on the offshore rocks,' he explained. 'A lot of bodies were washed ashore and brought up from the beach by the locals. The sad thing is that because nobody knew who they belonged to they were mostly buried in the surrounding fields and not the kirkyard. What you saw was very unusual, but perhaps the corpses were stored in the chapel until somewhere could be found for them.'

Of course, all of this was macabre, ancient history so far as Jack Shepherd from Bristol was concerned when he booked himself into a farmhouse B&B in the autumn of 2006. He had been heading south from Edinburgh, and decided to turn off the A1 just north of Dunbar on a whim. The sun was sinking in the west when he arrived in the farmyard and by eight o'clock it had become dark. Disinclined to go to bed so early, he set off for a stroll in the night air.

The wind was southerly and a full moon hung like a medallion over the North Sea. The moon path was effervescent as Jack followed the path along the clifftops. Entranced by the sheer drama of the scene, he somehow failed to notice the steep bank of mist building up, untouched by the moon's reflection.

Immersed in the moment, Jack breathed in the spectacle, oblivious to the shadows that were swallowing the shoreline. 'Nights like this should be cherished,' he muttered to himself, regretful that he was on his own. Overhead, he could see Jupiter and Saturn. He wished that he knew more about astronomy. On a night such as this, it was as if every star in the sky had come out for his benefit alone.

As such thoughts preoccupied him, two large horses unexpectedly loomed out of the darkness, their necks held down with rope and flickering lanterns swinging seaward from their backs.

Jack stepped back open-mouthed as they lumbered past, accompanied by the heavy figure of a man. Out at sea yet another light soon appeared, faint then flaring sharply as it moved swiftly towards the coast.

The crash, when it came, was chilling; a huge, splintering blast accompanied by an eerie scream of voices. From the cliff edge, Jack momentarily caught a glimpse of the fractured hulk of a sailing ship. Deeply shaken by the sight, he turned on his heels and raced back to the farmhouse to summon help.

When at last he burst into the front parlour, he found the farmer and his wife ensconced in front of their television. They listened patiently as he outlined the full horror of what had occurred. 'There's been a terrible accident. I think it's a shipwreck,' he blurted out. 'We've got to get help.'

The farmer's wife glanced anxiously at her husband. 'Best call the coastguard or best not?' she murmured calmly, with a trace of resignation in her voice.

The farmer rose grudgingly from his comfy armchair and pulled on his jacket. 'Best have a look first,' he said grumpily.

As Jack retraced his movements it was clear the farmer was unimpressed. The mist had by now dispersed and in the moonlight it was once again possible to make out the features of the shoreline. Jack had expected to hear more cries for help but the only sound to be heard was the hush of the surf.

'It was down there,' he said excitedly, pointing towards the cove.

The farmer shook his head. 'There's nothing we can do about it tonight,' he said.

Jack was speechless. 'But it was terrible,' he protested. 'We've got to do something. People were drowning.'

'What exactly did you see?' asked the farmer, sharply rounding on him. 'Was it a wee sailing yacht or one of those big cabin cruisers? Look away down there by the rocks. The tide's gone way beyond them. There's nothing there now. It'll have been the Pagans you saw the night, and they're long gone.'

Jack stared at him in bewilderment. 'What do you mean, it was the Pagans I saw?'

'Come away to the house, and I'll explain,' said the farmer.

On reaching the farmhouse, Jack reluctantly followed the old man into the kitchen where, not too reluctantly, he accepted a tumbler of single malt.

'Long ago in the days of merchant shipping, the sea traffic from the trade routes of Scotland to England and the Low Countries – Holland and Belgium – all of it passed this way,' the farmer began. 'In that time there lived hereabouts a colony of ungodly souls. Fowk were feared of them and called them the Pagans of Scoughall. Land pirates they were. On stormy nights, when the haar rolled in, they preyed on passing ships.

'On stormy nights, the men led their horses out onto the cliffs and marched them back and forth with lanterns tied to their necks. Ships far out on the ocean would catch sight of the lights and, thinking them boats at anchor, turn landward for shelter. Many a poor mariner came to grief on those rocks. Come the dawn, the Pagans claimed their spoils.'

'But surely nothing like that goes on nowadays?' said Jack, incredulous. The farmer and his wife looked at him in pity.

'Not the now,' said the farmer. 'But you'll no' be the first to catch a sight of the Pagans of Scoughall, and you'll no' be the last.'

Jack stared at the couple in disbelief. 'Are you telling me that what I saw tonight took place in another century?' he gasped, incredulous.

'Go down to the bay on the morrow to see for yourself,' said the old man. 'In the meantime, get yourself a good night's sleep. There's nothing you can do for those poor lost wretches the night.'

Upstairs, enveloped in his duvet, Jack slept fitfully. As soon as daybreak penetrated the curtains of his room, he was up and out of the farmhouse door. Outside, the air was fresh and dry and it hit him like a tonic as he strode along the pathway. On the beach below, he found the usual litter of driftwood, domestic refuse and plastic containers. Seagulls circled high above. There was no sign of a wrecked ship. Everything appeared to be as it should be, calm and undisturbed.

Over breakfast, the voice of the farmer's wife was sympathetic. 'Consider what you saw last night to be a privilege, son,' she said in a kindly voice. 'It's a rare treat for an outsider to be given a sight of auld lang syne.'

11

VISIONS FROM THE PAST

Because I could not stop for Death,
He kindly stopped for me;
The carriage held but just ourselves
And Immortality.

Emily Dickinson, 'The Chariot' (1890)

Domestic objects are as prone to conundrum as flesh and blood. Have you ever wondered about those who previously slept in an antique bed, coveted an Old Master hanging on a wall, or made showy use of a fine china tea service? Whose hands were they that once lovingly caressed that piece of fine Georgian silver? How many centuries have been chimed into oblivion by that grandfather clock?

Angus Laurie has been in the antiques trade for over thirty-five years and known both good times and bad. 'I've picked up some strange items and a bargain or two in my time, I can tell you,' he told me, 'but nothing quite like the high-backed Orkney chair I found way back at Kerr & McAllister's. I wasn't really that interested in it when I first saw it, but then something made me look again and I thought, why not?'

The chair was knocked down for remarkably little and Angus removed it to the shop he was then occupying on Great Western

Road. 'It was a bit like a cocoon,' he said. 'It had the usual straw back. I dated it as Victorian although maybe it was a bit later, around the turn of the century. On inspection, I have to say it was a bit worn and scruffy-looking, but I reckoned it'd look good on display once I'd patched it up a bit.'

Sales of antiques took off during the late 1990s, and Angus soon found himself making a tidy profit as Glasgow home-owners became more period conscious. However, an Orkney chair, despite its visual compatibility with the designs of Charles Rennie Mackintosh, was not considered a particularly desirable item, at least not at the price Angus had placed on it. 'I didn't want it to end up in some student flat,' he explained. 'It was too good for that.'

As the weeks passed, the chair remained in the corner of the shop and although the occasional customer commented upon it, nobody made Angus an offer. That was until one Thursday evening when just as he was on the point of closing up, an old man wearing a cloth cap and a heavy tweed overcoat entered the emporium and strode directly over to the chair.

'That's it,' he said in a lilting northern accent. 'That's my chair.'

Angus smiled to himself. 'Your chair?' he asked. 'How come?'

'I wove that straw my very self when I was a lad,' the man informed him.

Angus studied the stranger more closely, attempting a guess at his age. His skin, he saw, resembled wrinkled parchment. A salt-and-pepper stubble framed his cheeks. He must be seventy? Eighty perhaps? No, he could not possibly be old enough to have made the chair. On the other hand, if he was genuinely intent on buying it, who was he, Angus, to argue?

'How much?' asked the man.

'£350,' said Angus.

The old man chuckled. 'I'll take it,' he said.

Angus could barely conceal his amazement. 'Do you have transport?' he asked. 'If you live nearby I could have it delivered.'

'Nae problem,' replied the man. 'I'll leave it until the morrow.'

Angus wondered about that. He had lost sales before when folk had promised to return, but under the circumstances there seemed to be no alternative.

'OK. I open at 11 a.m.,' he said. 'But I'll need a deposit if you're serious.'

'You can have the lot,' said the old man, extracting a wad of well-worn Scottish bank notes from his overcoat pocket. 'You'll find it all there,' he added, handing him the money with a wrinkled hand.

'Good to do business with you,' said Angus hesitantly, as the old man took his leave.

'You're welcome,' came the response.

For no particular reason, Angus found himself unable to discard the image of the old man in the heavy tweed coat. Having closed the shutters, he made himself a cup of coffee and settled himself down in the Orkney chair. It was the first time he had actually made use of it, and, as he lowered himself into its womb-like enclosure, everything around him began to shift and change.

Gone were the papered shop walls hung with prints and bric-a-brac. The front counter and random pieces of Chippendale, the Georgian sideboards, tables and brass fenders were no more. Instead, Angus now found himself in a spartan room, its stone walls dimly lit by the flickering of an open peat fire. The floor upon which his feet rested was flagstone and cold, and crudely inserted into the walls on either side of the fireplace were two bunk beds.

Angus blinked. He must be hallucinating, he concluded. He blamed it on the strength of the black South American coffee in his mug. Then he noticed that the old man had returned, but no longer wore the heavy coat. Instead, he was warming himself in front of the fire in a linen shirt, his baggy tweed trousers supported by string braces.

And the old man was not alone. Seated in a high-backed Orkney chair identical to the one Angus was occupying himself was a woman with a heavy shawl draped over her shoulders. Her coarse brown hair was tied back in a bun, and she seemed preoccupied with her knitting.

Gone was the outside noise of traffic heading into the centre of Glasgow and west towards Dumbarton. Instead, Angus heard only the strength of the wind, a vast, ceaseless roar that pounded the senses as the peat in the fireplace flared and smoked.

The man seemed younger, he thought, although still rough and unkempt. The woman, whose face had a shiny pink surface, must presumably be of a similar vintage. There was a dusty, otherworldly look about the two of them. It was all far too peculiar for Angus to get his head around.

Then, as quickly as the vision had emerged, everything returned to normal. In a state of disbelief, Angus hastily pulled himself out of the high-backed chair and strode into the back shop to pour the remains of his coffee into the sink. Having locked the doors and switched on the alarm system, he headed home.

Never an early riser, it was around 11.15 the next morning when Angus opened up the shop, and it was only then that it crossed his mind that his visitor of the night before might have already been and gone. This was exactly the thought he was turning over when he closed the shop door behind him and realised something was wrong.

Everything else was in its place, but he saw, to his horror, that the high-backed Orkney chair had gone. Appalled, he looked about, wildly checking the windows and locks for signs of a break-in. No, everything with the exception of the chair was exactly as it had been left the previous day.

It defied explanation. It was absurd. What on earth was he to say to the old man when he returned to collect his chair? That it had vanished overnight? He would think him crazy, and there was the small matter of the payment. Angus would have no alternative but to give it back.

Momentarily, he contemplated calling in the police, but there was no evidence of a break-in. The shop door had definitely been locked; the windows shuttered. Angus was utterly baffled. The chair had definitely been in its place when he had last seen it.

All of that day and over the weeks and months that followed, Angus anxiously awaited the return of the old man. Every second day he rehearsed what he would say to him and speculated as to how he might react. A year passed and the lease of the shop in Great Western Road came to an end. Angus moved premises. He never saw the old man or the high-backed Orkney chair ever again.

Time-slips manifest themselves in a great many ways. Sometimes you see something; sometimes you do not. The past and the present and the future overlap seamlessly, but every now and then something goes wrong.

'Nae man can tether time or tide', is a favourite quote from Robert Burns's *Tam o' Shanter*, and it is therefore perhaps all the more appropriate that one of the more contrary examples of chronology I have come across should have occurred within a few miles of the bard's birthplace.

Molly Peaston is the locations editor for a well-known London-based homes and interiors magazine, and comes regularly to Scotland to seek out stylish country houses to write about and photograph. Having made several visits to the west coast, she made contact with the late James Hunter Blair, owner of Blairquhan, an imposing William Burn neo-Greek masterpiece near Maybole. Ever the generous host, Hunter Blair enthusiastically invited her to lunch and she set off from Glasgow in her hire car.

Never particularly good at following directions, Molly decided she had travelled the requisite distance when she arrived at a lodge and some imposing gates which, according to her calculations, must have been those of Blairquhan.

The driveway was typical: narrow, pitted with pot holes and flanked on either side by ditches and a tangle of bushes and trees. It seemed to go on forever until, turning a bend, she could see ahead of her a fine Palladian house. 'Wow,' she thought to herself.

Excited at her find, she stopped the car immediately below the front steps, and, having climbed them, eagerly tugged the bell-pull on the right of the front door. In the distance, she could hear a hollow clanging sound, but there was no response. She tried again, once more without success. Noticing that the door stood slightly ajar, she gave it a gentle push and stepped inside. 'It was amazingly palatial, with a wonderful high ceiling,' she recalled afterwards. 'On the walls on either side of the vestibule were stags' antlers and sporting trophies.'

Molly called out to announce her presence, and, after a short wait, a middle-aged woman appeared. 'I'm here to take photographs,' Molly informed her, at which the woman nodded and showed her into a spacious drawing room furnished with chintz-covered sofas and lavishly hung ancestral portraits. When Molly turned to ask what she should do next, the woman was no longer there.

'Ah well, I thought to myself, I might as well get on with it,' Molly told me later.

Exploring the rooms, Molly snapped away with her Instamatic camera to record everything she thought would interest her editor who, if she liked what she saw, would almost certainly commission a professional set of pictures from one of the magazine's freelance contributors.

'I was starting to feel hungry so I went to see if I could find the woman I'd met in the hall,' said Molly. 'I called out, hoping she'd hear me, but there was just nobody around. Finally, I thought I'd have a go at telephoning Jamie on my mobile. After all, he had invited me to lunch, and although I wasn't expecting him to come up with a full-blown luncheon, it seemed a bit odd he hadn't put in an appearance to welcome me. A bowl of soup would have done just fine.'

When Jamie answered her call he sounded puzzled. 'I was loyally expecting you at least an hour ago,' he told her. 'I thought you'd probably got lost.'

'No, I'm here already,' she replied. 'I've been going around the house taking photographs. I hope that's OK?'

There was a silence on the other end of the phone.

'I don't understand,' said Jamie at last. 'I've been here all morning. I would have seen you.'

A feeling of apprehension began to dawn on Molly.

'Does your house have large pillars at the door, and a large marble hallway?'

'Yes,' replied Jamie.

'Do you have a housekeeper who wears a calf-length patterned skirt? And is there a wide staircase with a full-length portrait of a woman on the landing?'

'Not that I'm aware of,' said Jamie.

'Oh my God, I think I'm in the wrong house,' said Molly.

'Describe it to me,' continued Jamie, falling silent as she did so.

As best she could, Molly filled in the details. When she had finished, she thought Jamie sounded strangely distant.

'I think you should go back down the drive you arrived on and follow the road signs south towards Maybole,' he told her calmly. 'Keep your mobile phone on so I can talk you in.'

Molly followed his instructions and much to her relief arrived at Blairquhan some twenty minutes later. Sitting down to enjoy a bowl of soup and a glass of wine, Jamie asked her to slowly go over again where she had been and what she had seen.

'It can't be more than twenty miles from here,' she told him and he nodded thoughtfully. When she had finished, he seemed to be confused.

'I think the place you've been describing to me is probably Montgomerie House, which is next to Tarbolton,' he told her.

'Thank goodness for that,' she said. 'I thought I was going mad.'

'There's only one problem,' continued Jamie. 'Montgomerie House, which used to belong to the Arthur family, loyal friends of mine, was sold in the 1960s. Shortly after that it was burned to the ground in a fire. There is nothing left of it. You can just make out where it was by the markings in the field, but everything else has gone.'

Molly looked askance. 'But I have photographs of the rooms!' she protested.

To be certain, the two of them later that day retraced Molly's journey back to Tarbolton and, sure enough, as soon as they turned into the drive, she saw that the mansion had vanished. Thankfully Jamie was highly amused at her predicament.

'Make sure you send me the photographs when you get them developed,' he reminded her as she set off in her car again towards Glasgow. 'Now those will be interesting!'

Remember that this was in the early days of digital photography and before the science was improved, most glossy magazines still preferred to use film. As soon as she was back in her office, therefore, Molly handed over her spools to be processed, but to her bitter disappointment, and eternal bewilderment, when her pictures were returned they were found to be over-exposed. Virtually nothing in the images was identifiable, only the faint outline of a large exterior building, a washed-out interior staircase and a series of seemingly empty spaces. All of the pictures were two-tone, with a yellowish milky substance seeping over the surfaces. It was as if they had been dropped in acid.

'Nothing like that has ever happened to me before,' Molly informed Jamie over the telephone. 'You must think I'm completely off my trolley. But I was there. I really was. I know I was. I couldn't have made it up.'

Jamie was sympathetic. 'That sort of thing happens a lot in Ayrshire,' he said kindly.

12

A STATE OF GRACE

But let me breathe my heart's warm flame,
Aneath yon auld tree's aged frame,
Where friendship past may justly claim
A silent tear,
To trace ilk rudely-sculptured name
O' comrades dear.

Richard Gall, *Address to Haddington* (1819)

The village of Sauchie in Clackmannanshire consists of a quiet, close-knit community, and it was into this safe environment that the eleven-year-old Virginia Campbell arrived with her mother in 1960. They had come to live with her elder brother and his family, whilst their father remained in Ireland to sell the family farm in Donegal.

It proved a major upheaval for a young girl. Moreover, Virginia desperately missed her only friend, Annie, and her dog, Toby. The situation was further exacerbated when her mother took employment at a boarding house in Dollar. Virginia not only found herself obliged to share a bed with her younger niece Margaret, but having to attend a new school.

All of this led to an escalating sense of unhappiness and

frustration, and on a November night, both of the girls came racing downstairs from their bedroom to inform their startled parents that they had heard a strange noise in the room above. Their arrival at the foot of the stairs coincided with what sounded like a bouncing ball following them.

Over the week that followed, loud knocking sounds were heard after the girls had gone to bed and the local minister, the Reverend TW Lund, was approached for his advice. On visiting the house after the girls had been sent to bed, he too heard the loud knockings and suggested that perhaps they came from the head board. When a heavy linen chest began to rock from side to side before rising from the floor and moving in the direction of the bed, it became obvious that something needed to be done about it fast. The following night there were further knocking sounds. A china vase moved. An apple rose from out of a bowl and a sewing machine started to whir all on its own.

Such bizarre occurrences were not restricted to the family's home. In Virginia's schoolroom, her teacher, Margaret Stewart, witnessed a desk rise off the ground, and when Virginia approached it, a blackboard pointer started to vibrate before falling onto the floor. Virginia was becoming increasingly dazed and hysterical. Anyone could see that medical help was urgently required.

Neither Dr WH Nisbet nor Dr William Logan, the local practitioners, had encountered anything like this before, and they decided to install a tape recorder and movie camera in the girls' bedroom to capture sound and movement, including Virginia becoming hysterical. Meanwhile, the Reverend Lund and three of his colleagues prayed for divine intervention.

The turmoil lasted several weeks. Investigators were baffled until, as soon as Virginia was reunited with her dog Toby, the noises stopped.

Shortly before he emigrated to Canada in 1970 to become director of the Toronto-based New Horizons Research Foundation, the well-known geneticist and university lecturer Dr George Owen was asked for his opinion and attributed the entire episode to prepubescent energy brought on by Virginia's homesickness and shyness. There was no trickery involved. The Campbell family appeared to be loving and stable.

Which all goes to prove that the power of the subconscious is a formidable opponent when aroused.

Exorcism is far more regularly practised than is generally thought. In Chapter Two, I mentioned Gordon McNeill-Wilkie and the cleansing of Ashintully Castle. Similarly, Bill Caffrey's involvement with Dunans Castle in Chapter One. More commonly, however, it is the Church that is called upon to expel demons. The New Testament refers to exorcisms in the context of the miracles of Jesus Christ, but while Catholic, Eastern Orthodox, Islamic and Protestant faiths all acknowledge the skills employed, I have generally found most members of the priesthood extremely reluctant to commit themselves on the subject.

And if anything, the release of the 1973 Hollywood film *The Exorcist*, based on the novel by William Peter Blatty, made matters worse. In Germany, two priests were given suspended jail sentences for performing the exorcism ritual sixty-seven times on a mentally ill sixteen-year-old girl. The scandal surrounding this was in 2005 the basis for yet another Hollywood blockbuster, *The Exorcism of Emily Rose*, and it was this that allegedly prompted the Catholic Church to introduce training procedures. As recently as 2007, Pope Benedict XVI issued instructions for exorcism squads of trained priests to be set up to tackle a rise in Satanism.

While not prepared to be either named or cross-examined on the subject, a senior figure in the Church of Scotland reassures me that although he has certainly encountered some bizarre situations, most of the invocation work he has been called upon to perform is pretty mundane.

'When it comes to disturbed human beings, psychiatrists and doctors usually know what they are doing,' he said. 'Only now and then do we come up against something genuinely ugly. Mostly it's folk in their own homes who feel threatened by poltergeists, or an oppressive atmosphere. A blessing usually does the trick. I'm not prepared to go into detail, but so far I have never had to go back and repeat the ritual.'

A typical story is that of the Lumley family, who were filled with excitement at the prospect of moving into a converted farm steading. At least, that was the impression given by Mike and Poppy to their friends, but their daughters, Mandy and Jennifer, were less enthused at the prospect.

Previously, they had occupied a three-bedroom tenement flat in the west end of Glasgow and now they were the proud occupants of a period conversion close to the Falls of Clyde in Lanarkshire. It was what Mike and Poppy had always dreamed of, a step up the property ladder, but from fourteen-year-old Mandy, and Jennifer, aged sixteen, came mixed reactions.

While both girls warmed to the idea of a bigger house providing more space for them to escape from their parents, neither was exactly overwhelmed by the prospect of living out of town. Both were enrolled at the same fee-paying school and the greater majority of their schoolfriends lived near it. No longer would they be able to casually meet up to go to the cinema after school hours, or chill out at a favourite café at weekends. Added to which, there was the extra effort of a daily commute, although it only involved a half-hour car run. Fortunately, both father and mother worked in close proximity to the school, and both drove.

So for them, at least, it was not considered a big issue. But for Mandy and Jennifer, the move involved a huge compromise in their accustomed lifestyle.

'You're taking us to Siberia,' complained Jennifer once she had thought it through. The truth was that while she liked the idea of living in a posh house, she disliked the idea of the country: endless fields full of smelly animals like cows and horses and, above all, the absence of human beings. Where were the shops and the fun places to hang out?

So to start off with, the Lumley family's move to the Lanarkshire countryside was not without disharmony, commencing with Mandy and Jennifer quarrelling over the size of their bedrooms. As the eldest, Jennifer demanded the one on the first level over-looking the driveway, the one her parents had designated as a guest room. Mandy wanted it too, but eventually accepted one with an en-suite shower to the rear of the house, overlooking the river. Eventually, Mike and Poppy gave in to Jennifer, and she was allowed the room she wanted. Their own bedroom, with a small balcony overlooking open fields, was on the far side of the steading, which meant both daughters could make as much noise as they wanted, within reason.

As he made his tour of inspection, Mike congratulated himself on his purchase. With only one previous owner since the conversion, the architectural and design finishes throughout were as good as its gets. The kitchen range was state-of-the-art. There was double glazing and loft insulation. The levels had been re-timbered in polished pine. What more could you possibly ask for in terms of blending the best of the old with the new?

Yet Mike still had an uneasy feeling that the asking price had been too cheap. This was several years before the credit crisis of 2008–10, and at a time when property prices were soaring stead-ily. Although mortgaged up to the hilt, he had never in his wildest dreams believed he would be able to afford such a property. Both he and his agent had been amazed when the seller agreed to a figure well below the asking price. Apparently he was leaving the country and wanted a quick sale.

Poppy had been ecstatic when she'd heard the news. It was everything she had always wanted, a house with a garden in the country. 'I've only ever had a window box before,' she confided to her jealous girlfriends at work.

But when the removal vans had finally come and gone, and the Lumleys were installed in their new home, the task of sorting everything out seemed colossal. Jennifer, for example, wanted broadband for her computer; Mandy wanted Sky television. Poppy looked wistfully at her town wardrobe of smart office work-wear outfits, party frocks and designer shoes. 'We really are living in the country now,' she sighed. 'It'll be Hunter wellies and moleskin breeks from now on.'

It took them a full week to get the household up and running. It was the school holidays so at least the girls were at home all day to help out, and Mike and Poppy had taken a week off. Although Jennifer talked endlessly on her mobile phone and complained incessantly that she had better things to do, it all eventually fell into place. By the following weekend, a sense of normality had returned to the family's routine.

Normality of the sort that Jennifer accused Mandy of stealing her make-up and favourite T-shirt, an allegation which Mandy vehemently denied. The next day, there was a similar row. Mandy had been in Jennifer's room again, this time using her shampoo.

When Poppy went into Jennifer's room in the afternoon to see for herself, she called out to Mike in concern. The girls had gone out for a walk and she led Mike directly over to Jennifer's dressing table.

'Somebody's been smoking in here,' she said.

Sure enough a lingering pungent odour was immediately apparent.. 'Don't be ridiculous, neither of the girls smoke,' said Mike. 'You know that.'

He himself had given up long before he had met Poppy, but he knew that her dislike of smoking stemmed from her father's habit of forty cigarettes a day.

'Well, how else do you explain the smell?' she snapped, gesticulating as she did so. 'This is all I need!'

When Jennifer returned to face a barrage of hostile questioning, she flared up in resentment. 'You know I don't smoke,' she screamed at her parents. 'It must have been Mandy when she was going through my things!'

'I've never been near your stupid things!' shouted Mandy in response.

Their parents looked at each other helplessly. 'We'll leave it for now,' said Mike, who hated any kind of row or confrontation.

All the same, when Jennifer set off to the village the following day, Poppy sneaked back into her room and once again, there was a lingering smell. 'Do you know what?' said Mike when she summoned him. 'That's not cigarette smoke. That's pipe tobacco.'

'Don't talk nonsense,' said his wife. 'Why would Jennifer smoke a pipe?'

The idea seemed so absurd that they both burst out laughing, which to some extent relieved the tension. But not for long. 'Well, if Jennifer hasn't started smoking a pipe, who has?' said Poppy, rounding on her husband.

'You surely don't think I . . .'

'No, of course not, but somebody has definitely been smoking in this room,' she said, throwing open the windows to let in the outside air. As she did so, she ran her finger along the sill and lifted the tip to her nose. 'I suppose we should be thankful that it's not marijuana. We'll just have to keep our eyes open.'

Although Jennifer was entering that appalling teenage phase of mandatory rebellion, she was an intelligent girl who, despite silly crushes on boys and hating to be told what to do when she always knew better, genuinely loved her parents. As she lay in bed at night, a thousand fantasies passed through her thoughts, the majority involving Roy Spooner, a rising star of the school's football team. She had recently been to the cinema with him to see *Lord of the Rings*, but now that she had moved out of town she wondered if he would want to have anything to do with her ever again. She closed her eyes trying to imagine him leaning over her to kiss her goodnight. When she opened them she thought that she could smell him, but then realised that it was not Roy at all that stood before her. It was a horrid old man who smelled of tobacco smoke.

Jennifer screamed and, hurling herself out of bed, raced along the corridor to her parents' bedroom. When finally they managed to make some sense of what she was telling them, both Mike and Poppy went to investigate. The bedroom was empty, but the air was filled with the smell of stale tobacco smoke. 'I just can't understand it,' said Mike, examining the radiators and opening up the fitted wall cupboards. 'It has to be coming from somewhere.'

Yet there was clearly nobody there. Poppy was all for calling the police, but Mike restrained her. 'What on earth do we say to them? That there's been a break-in when all of the doors and windows are shut? Let's leave it until the morning.'

For the remainder of that night Jennifer occupied the guest bedroom, and the next day moved her belongings to her new quarters. On his way to work Mike looked in on the nearest police station and was seen by a lady officer who listened attentively to what he had to say.

'What age did you say your daughter was?' she asked.

'I didn't,' he replied. 'But she's sixteen.'

'I see,' said the policewoman. 'Has anything like this happened before?'

'No, never.'

'And you say that you only moved into the house ten days ago?'

'Yes.'

The woman paused and put aside her pencil. 'I shouldn't really be telling you this, but there's been a problem at this address before. I take it the previous owner didn't mention anything about it to you?'

Mike looked puzzled. 'No. I never met him.'

The policewoman smiled and consulted the contents of a file she had withdrawn from a filing cabinet. 'It appears that there have been several previous incidents reported. All of them of – er – should I say, a supernatural nature.'

'What are you saying?' said Mike astonished. 'That the steading is haunted?'

The policewoman looked at him sympathetically. 'It would appear so,' she said.

'Don't tell me you believe in all that stuff?' said Mike.

'We come across all sorts of strange goings-on in our work,' she replied with stoicism.

Having arranged that somebody from the station would pay them a visit in the early evening, Mike drove to work where he telephoned Poppy to report on what had taken place. As he had expected, the pitch of her voice rose in irritation. 'Is that the best they can do?' she responded angrily.

That evening the Reverend Hamilton of St Matthew's Church paid them a visit. 'I received a call from the police this afternoon asking if I would look in on you,' he explained when Mike opened the front door and invited him in. 'I understand that Gideon Somerville has been causing you a few problems.'

'No, I don't think so,' said Mike. 'Who is Gideon Somerville?'

The Reverend Hamilton shook his head. 'On that basis, I conclude that nobody has told you about him?'

Mike turned to Poppy, and she shrugged her shoulders. Meanwhile, Jennifer and Mandy had entered the room. The minister, informally dressed without the collar of his calling, nodded to them as they sat down on either side of the fireplace. 'I wouldn't want you to have nightmares about what I'm about to tell you,' he continued.

'It's all right,' said Poppy confidently. 'We don't hide anything from our children.'

'Quite right. Quite right,' said the Reverend Hamilton. 'All the same, it's not a pretty story.'

A while ago, he explained to them, back in the 1970s it was, the steading which they now occupied was used for storing agricultural equipment by Gideon Somerville. An unmarried tenant farmer in his forties, he late in life became engaged to a local girl whom he had previously employed to cook and clean for him. According to local gossip, she had really set her cap at him and bossed him about something terrible, always fussing over how he dressed and, in particular, encouraging him to stop smoking. On the eve of their wedding, however, she vanished without a trace.

'Her family and Gideon searched high and low for her, but she was never found,' said the minister. 'Then the rumours started. Some claimed she'd gone off abroad; others whispered he'd done her in. Gideon was notorious for having a bad temper. Most folk around here were amazed she should even have given him a second glance. But then love can be a funny old business, whichever way you look at it.

'Anyway, the police were contacted and Gideon was questioned, but seemed genuinely distraught at her absence. Nobody could prove anything and eventually the investigation was called off. After that, Gideon became a recluse and began drinking heavily.

'He kept his distance from the village and the folk around here avoided him. I can remember coming here to see him when I first started my ministry at St Matthew's. It was a complete waste of time. His appearance alone was a shock. He resembled an old tramp, unshaven and unwashed. He reeked of pipe tobacco. I think he must have chewed it.

'Although I hate to concede defeat, I knew at once there was nothing I could do for him. He wouldn't allow me the light of day and made it perfectly clear I was unwelcome on his land. So, much to my shame, I left him to get on with whatever it was he did. The next thing I heard was that he'd died of liver failure or some such disease. I was genuinely sorry to hear that. Nobody deserves to die alone, and when they had tracked down his nearest relative, the lawyers asked me to preside over his burial service.'

The Reverend Hamilton shook his head sadly. 'A sorry soul. And that would have been the end of it, except when it came to light that the rumours about the girl had been right all along.'

Mike exchanged glances with Poppy and their daughters. 'You mean that . . . ?'

The minister nodded. 'He had indeed murdered his fiancée.'

'But apart from the smell of tobacco, what does that have to do with us?' asked Mike after a shocked silence.

'Ah,' said the minister. 'I'll explain.'

For over forty years, the scandalmongers had insisted Gideon Somerville had done away with his bride on the night before their wedding. But it was not until the farm and steadings were sold for development that the terrible truth emerged. During demolition work, the diggers had unearthed the skeleton of a thirty-year-old woman wrapped in a blanket and buried under the floor of an outhouse. Through forensic and tooth analysis, it was confirmed that these were the remains of the missing housekeeper.

'And all those years he'd had her under his feet less than a stone's throw from the farm,' said the minister, shaking his head.

'But from what I've been told, the old farm house was on the other side of the river in the new housing development,' said Mike. 'Why should Gideon turn up here?'

The minister faced him. 'Aye,' he said, 'but this is where he used to come to escape from her nagging. Locals say he came over here for a smoke of an evening, and after she disappeared, he slept here. Guilty conscience, no doubt. He needed to distance himself from the scene of his crime.'

'So what you're telling us is that our home is haunted by a horrid old farmer who murdered his future wife and still likes to go out for a smoke at night?' said Poppy, shuddering.

'Exactly.'

'And you mean to say the previous owner knew about this and didn't tell us?'

'Under the circumstances, would you?'

The Lumleys, as a unit, were speechless. Then Mike spoke. 'So is there anything we can do about it?'

'That's exactly why I'm here tonight,' said the Reverend Hamilton.

The exorcism that followed was conducted along the prescribed pattern of prayers and a leading towards the light. 'Especially difficult when the soul of the departed is being sent to Hell,' explained the Reverend Hamilton with a grimace. 'Knowing what we know, there's no guarantee it will work.'

However, by the following month all traces of the putrid tobacco smell had dispersed. The story of Gideon Somerville nevertheless continued to bother Mike and Poppy, especially as they knew where and when it had taken place, and in living memory. 'It'll be impossible if and when we decide to sell up and move on,' complained Mike.

'Let's cross that bridge when we come to it,' Poppy reassured him.

Of course, there was an up-side to this gruesome saga. Jennifer remained in her new bedroom and never again accused her sister Mandy of interfering with her make-up and clothes. Moreover, both girls revelled in telling the story of Gideon Somerville to their school friends who, despite being dependent on public transport, were all too eager to travel out of town to stay in the guest room at weekends.

Six months later Roy Spooner was promoted to captain of the school football team and he and Jennifer became what is nowadays generally known as a serious item.

'Living in the country's not so bad after all,' she informed her mother as the family sat down to dinner one night. 'It's not nearly as boring as I thought it would be.'

13

THE STUFF THAT DREAMS
ARE MADE OF

Deep into that darkness peering, long I stood there,
wondering, fearing,
Doubting, dreaming dreams no mortal ever dared to
dream before

Edgar Allan Poe, 'The Raven' (1845)

It was well over twenty years ago that an elderly lady of my acquaintance confessed to me that in her sleep she had seen fire falling from the sky over southern Scotland. Her nightmares started in the summer of 1988, six months before Pan Am Flight 103 exploded over the small town of Lockerbie.

Dreams are common to everyone, although only occasionally do we recall their content in detail. Watch a sleeping figure while he or she is dreaming and the eyelids and mouth twitch and flicker and the eyebrows furrow. Something involuntary is taking place.

Jolyon Spence from Moulin in Perthshire was in her mid-twenties when she experienced a series of vivid dreams. 'They always came around dawn in that half-sleep when the ghosts start to appear,' she said.

'I was in a car with a man at the wheel and two children in the back seats. We were all being very happy and jolly, although it was pouring with rain outside. The car was heading along some nondescript Highland road with trees on either side. I don't remember the rain being particularly heavy but all of a sudden there was this great roaring noise and a mountain of rocks and mud came crashing down in front of us.'

Jolyon told me the nightmare repeated itself until she met her husband Ted. When they married in 1991, they stopped. Michael and Nicholas were born, and as they were growing up, she and Ted rented a house for the summer holidays at Killin in Perthshire.

'Mike and Nick absolutely adored it,' she recalled nostalgically. 'They got to sail and water ski on Loch Earn and their dad took them fishing. It was lots of fun, but one evening, it was my birthday and we'd been out to dinner at a local restaurant. We were travelling back through Lochearnhead when I suddenly had this awful sensation of impending doom. I looked at the road ahead of us and it was just exactly as it had been in my dream. It was raining. Ted was cracking jokes and the boys were laughing, and before I knew what was happening, there was a massive landslide. Fortunately, my husband slammed on the brakes and we swerved into a ditch.' Thankfully, nobody was hurt and they were not alone in their plight. Around fifty other motorists were trapped in their cars until a helicopter from RAF Kinloss arrived to fly them to safety. Heavy rain from the tropical storm Bonnie was blamed.

'It was a horrific shock at the time, and a miracle that we weren't all swept away,' said Jolyon with a shudder. 'But although I didn't exactly realise it at the time, it's reassuring to know I'd been forewarned, even if it was thirteen years before anything happened.'

Aside from warning, dreams can have a practical application.

Having been born and brought up beside the hamlet of Pencaitland, Avril Kirk is no outsider to East Lothian folklore, and today lives in the village of Humbie, where she has been researching her family tree.

One of her first discoveries was that her great-great-grandmother, Agnes Bone, had been born in Dunbar. Now, Avril already knew that Agnes's daughter, her great-grandmother, had been born illegitimately at Skateraw, a tiny coastal community, and because of this, she had begun her research in that area, but found nothing.

Disappointed, Avril had almost given up when one night she had a dream about a small harbour and heard a voice telling her to look to the left. 'I naturally assumed it was Skateraw Harbour,' she said.

The very next day she and her husband Malcolm set off to visit their granddaughter in Dunbar and because of the dream decided to make a diversion to Skateraw on the return journey.

'We were passing the old Parish Church when I suddenly felt an impulse to stop and have a look at the graveyard,' she recalled. 'For no particular reason, I found myself standing in front of the grave of George Robertson. I'd not come across any Robertsons in our family, and was about to move on when I noticed his wife's name was Agnes Bone!

'She must have married shortly after giving birth to my great-grandmother. By some unexpected chance I'd found her grave while looking for her birthplace!'

What turned out to be a rather more immediate vision of the future was experienced by an Edinburgh taxi-driver on a nightshift in the winter of 2002. Working nights can be very disorientating as it disrupts normal sleep patterns, but this cab driver, whom I shall call Bert, told me you get used to it. 'You just have to make yourself go to bed as soon as you knock off,' he said. 'The money is good, and, if you're feeling totally knackered, you can always pull over for a wee sleep.'

It was during one of these 'wee sleeps' that Bert had his first and probably his most startling premonition. 'Normally Saturday nights are hectic between midnight and two a.m., when things ease off,' he explained. 'It was early December. I'd taken the night before off for the wife's brother's engagement party. I was feeling a bit rough, so after I'd dropped a fare off at the Scotsman Hotel, I parked the cab in Blair Street, just off the High Street, for a wee bit of shut-eye.

'It was really weird,' he continued. 'I don't believe in all that psychic baloney, but I started getting all this stuff about a building on fire. I was walking along the Cowgate towards the Grassmarket, and a man ran past shouting out something about towering infernos. When I turned around, there was a wall of flame coming. I started running. The heat was suffocating and I woke up choking.'

When Bert woke up, he says everything in Blair Street was silent. At the foot of the hill he could see the Cowgate, but there was no one around. 'I looked at my watch and it was five a.m. I must have been asleep for at least a couple of hours.'

It was not until the following evening, however, that the Cowgate, under Edinburgh's South Bridge, ignited into flame. A fire had broken out in La Belle Angèle nightclub, rapidly spreading to the Gilded Balloon Fringe venue, part of the former 369 Art Gallery building. The flames quickly took hold of the adjoining terrace, lighting up the sky for miles around and smothering Edinburgh's Old Town in acrid smoke.

No fewer than nineteen fire crews, the majority from Lothian & Borders Fire Brigade, were called upon to get the blaze under control, and both the Cowgate and South Bridge remained closed for several days thereafter.

'I was away on the south side dropping a fare off at Prestonfield when I heard the news on the car radio,' said Bert. 'It made me feel pretty peculiar, I can tell you.'

Since then, Bert has had similar flashes of second sight, but is increasingly reluctant to talk about them. When I saw him five years ago, he told me how he had collected a bearded man with reddish hair in the Grassmarket and driven him to the Scottish Parliament building at Holyrood.

Bert had recognised him as Robin Cook, the Labour politician and former UK government minister. 'He told me he'd been having his portrait painted by a local artist and just been to see the finished work in her studio,' said Bert. 'He was a good bloke. I really took to him although I've never voted Labour in my life.'

Months later Bert had a dream in which he saw Cook standing with a woman on the summit of a high mountain. They were admiring the view when Cook collapsed. When Bert awoke, he dismissed the image from his mind. However, that very evening the news broke that Robin Cook had indeed died from a heart attack while climbing Ben Stack in Sutherland.

'It was deeply shocking,' said Bert. 'What staggered me most was he was only fifty-nine. I guess his opposition to the Iraq War must have really stressed him out.'

Although Bert more often than not considers his gift a curse, he has learned to live with it. 'I meet a lot of complete strangers and know at once when something bad is going to happen. What am I supposed to do about it? What can I do about it? If I warn them that something dreadful is about to happen, it'll only upset them and you can't interfere with fate. I don't know why I have these visions. I didn't ask for them.'

14

CASTLES IN THE AIR

In the case of the phantom car, however, the impatient driver, having waited for a minute or two, goes cautiously forward and finds absolutely nothing before him – the road is clear. The other car cannot have turned round and gone back the way it came, for there is no room to do so; it has simply disappeared.

Gavin Maxwell, *Raven Seek Thy Brother* (1968)

As much to do with their size as with their Gothic ostentation, Scotland's historic country houses, mansions and castles lend themselves unconditionally to tales of hauntings and spine-chilling spectral visitations. Overall, Scotland shares all the trappings of a Transylvanian film set. When a building is old or careworn it goes without saying that it holds secrets, but life, as we know, moves on. Gloom is a transitory condition, but sometimes it can come back to haunt us with a vengeance.

In Argyll, the current Laird of Lunga House at Craignish is the irrepressible Colin Lindsay-MacDougall, the latest in a long line of rumbustious seafarers who have occupied this strategic spot since the sixteenth century.

The MacDougalls, bitter enemies of Robert the Bruce, were

a constant force to be reckoned with, and with such a turbulent pedigree it is only to be expected that Lunga House has a few stories to tell. First-time visitors frequently remark on the front hallway being full of people when, in the reality of the moment, there is nobody there. Arriving home after a long drive, the laird's sister, Anne, recalls going straight into the morning room and finding it occupied by an animated crowd.

She was tired, and, assuming her brother was having a party, she reluctantly threaded her way across to the warmth of the fireplace. When she turned around, the room had emptied.

Sharply intelligent, Anne was also known to be prescient. Another such family anecdote involves her and her husband Jonathan; after their honeymoon in the Outer Isles, the two of them were invited to stay with some neighbours of her brother's at Ardfern. Their bedroom was to the rear of the house, and towards dawn, Jonathan was awoken by what he at first assumed to be car headlights shining onto the wall opposite their bed, casting shadows of tree branches.

Since there was no access for a car at the back of the house, he concluded that this had to be impossible. Sitting up in bed, he was further astonished when a piper emerged through the wall of an adjoining room. It was a military piper in full uniform, but although he appeared to be playing a set of bagpipes, there was no sound. The atmosphere in the room became leaden and oppressive. Jonathan looked on, not knowing what to do until, as fast as the image had revealed itself, it evaporated into the ether.

Anne, being in bed beside Jonathan, also witnessed the apparition, which she later described as emerging within a swirl of light. 'It was the sensation of doom that I found most unsettling,' she said afterwards. 'You felt that something really awful had happened.'

Anne's half-sister, Louise, is convinced that it had something to do with Anne's father, who had been an officer with the Argyll & Sutherland Highlanders. He had taken part in the invasion of Sicily during the First World War and had died from his wounds in an Italian prisoner-of-war camp. 'I think it was probably him trying to get a message through to her,' she said.

The majority of manifestations in old country houses concern the loss of loved ones.

South of the city of Aberdeen, close to the village of Ellon, is Haddo House, ancestral seat of the earls and marquesses of Aberdeen. Nowadays opened to the public by the National Trust for Scotland, its sumptuous Victorian interiors seem almost too comfortable to house a ghost.

But loss creates a vacuum. In 1909, Lord Archie, youngest son of the seventh earl, was killed in a car crash at the age of twenty-five.

Much loved, his body was brought home to Haddo for interment in the family chapel. His portrait, dressed as a pageboy when his father was Governor General of Canada, hangs on a wall, and there have been sightings of a young man fitting his description lurking in the shadows of the library in the north wing. Trust tour guides speak of hearing his footsteps in the corridors.

Another historic house maintained by the National Trust for Scotland stands on the outskirts of Forres in Morayshire. Brodie Castle has been the home of the family of the same name since they were given their lands in the twelfth century, but although known to have been one of Scotland's original Pictish/Celtic tribes, all of the early family records were incinerated when the original castle caught fire in 1645.

In 1727, Alexander, the nineteenth Brodie of Brodie, was appointed Lord Lyon King of Arms, a heraldic post directly accountable to the monarch, but successive generations have concentrated on improving their domestic inheritance and running out of money in the process, an all too common story among the Scottish aristocracy.

When Ninian Brodie and his wife Helen inherited the estate after the Second World War, therefore, they faced the problems which every twentieth-century stately home owner sooner or later has to confront. The costs involved in repairing and maintaining an ancient Scottish castle can be crippling.

Nevertheless, the Brodies set about restoring the old place with enthusiasm and brought up their children in a family wing before opening the main house to the paying public in 1972. It was around this time that Martin Hunt, founder of the Edinburgh-based public relations company Tartan Silk, was first invited to lunch and given a personal tour of the public rooms by Ninian.

Martin was enchanted by the twenty-fifth Laird of Brodie, a distinguished figure of great charm who had formerly been an actor with the Old Vic Theatre Company. Just as they were about to enter the dining room, however, Ninian was called away to answer a telephone call and suggested that Martin have a look at his mother's sitting room in his absence. In another turret, the room was sunny and elegant but, on entering, Martin found that one of the chairs was occupied by a soldier dressed in a light khaki uniform. In particular, he noticed that the man's boots were splashed with mud, a light clay in colour.

To begin with, he assumed he must have intruded upon a family member, but since the figure remained motionless and said nothing, Martin rapidly concluded that it must be a very cleverly made wax model, probably set up for the recent opening of the castle. He therefore made no mention of it over lunch.

In 1980, Brodie Castle was purchased by the National Trust for Scotland with an endowment from the Brodie family, and it was not until then that Martin made a return visit, accompanied by two young children whom he had briefed beforehand about the wax model.

'Everything was more or less exactly as I remembered it,' he recalls. 'Ninian asked for my opinion on the changes made by the National Trust, and I told him that we were disappointed not to see the wax model of the soldier in his mother's sitting room. He looked at me as if I were mad and said he had no idea what I was talking about. When I explained, he was adamant that there had never been a dummy in that room.

'But I'm certain it was there,' says Martin. 'I later asked Ninian's daughter Juliet about it, and she concurred with her father. There had never been anything of the sort in that room. So if it wasn't a dummy in uniform, who or what was it?'

When asked to describe the uniform Martin is adamant about it being khaki. In that case, it could therefore not have belonged to a Cumberland Redcoat from the 1745 Jacobite Rising; nor could it have been the Lord Lyon Brodie himself. The uniform was far more contemporary, which suggests a much more recent candidate.

In 1898, Captain Alastair Brodie was killed in action at Magersfontein in South Africa during the Boer War. He was aged twenty-eight and an Adjutant with the second Battalion, the Seaforth Highlanders. Seventeen years later, his younger brother Douglas was killed in action during the First World War. Both men would have worn khaki and both sons fit the description of the solitary figure in uniform whom Martin saw back in 1972.

To the south-east, as the glens of Angus finger into Perthshire, is Bamff House, where wild boars roam free in the tangled woodland and where the laird, Paul Ramsay, has recently introduced beavers into the river. Singularly remote from the maelstrom of urban existence, the estate has been compared to Jurassic Park, but yet again there is a story of a much-loved younger son who died fighting for king and country. His name was David Ramsay of the Scottish Horse Regiment, and he met his end during the Second World War, a tragedy from which his parents never fully recovered. Although the generations have moved on, his smiling face still looks out from a silver photograph frame in the drawing room. On the walls of his bedroom, his watercolour paintings of landscapes and owls perpetuate his memory.

Guests often sleep in David Ramsay's bedroom overnight. With its busy Colefax & Fowler wallpaper, it provides a compact and welcoming enough space in this most hospitable of households, but some are more sensitive to David's continuing presence than others.

Invited to stay for the weekend, an Edinburgh-based lawyer claims to have had his bedclothes ripped off as he slept. Sufficiently alarmed, he made a rapid departure the following morning and has never returned. He prefers not to talk about it but fortunately his host and hostess find the incident highly amusing.

'No, we didn't set him up,' I was told. 'He's just the sort of person who David would have enjoyed spooking.'

Family fortunes are capricious, as many of Scotland's oldest dynasties know only too well.

Nestling into a leafy ridge overlooking the Carse of the River Tay as it wends its stately way from Perth towards Dundee is Fingask Castle which, with a few hiccups, has been the home of the Threipland family for 500 years. Staunch Jacobite supporters, their estate was confiscated by the Crown after the 1715 Rising, but repurchased in 1783 by Sir Stuart Threipland using his wife's money. After that, it was held by their descendants until the 1920s, when it was disposed of by the present owner's grandfather.

The Threiplands' unwise political choices have meant that over the past 400 years they have lost and retrieved Fingask on four occasions. Having been sold and bought back again in 1968 and 1993, the present owners, Andrew and Helen Murray Threipland, are all the more determined to secure the future of their family home.

With its ancient topiaries, statues and medieval Holy Well of St Peter, the Fingask estate has therefore been transformed into a popular venue for wedding celebrations held in a purpose-built marquee in full view of the castle. Andrew and Helen also host the Fingask Follies, a delightful series of annual evening enter-tainments which take place in the castle's drawing room.

But Fingask was a very different place back in the early 1920s, when the estate was bought by Sir John Henderson-Stewart, sole proprietor of Alexander Stewart & Sons, Scotch Whisky Distillers of Dundee. As the Deputy Chairman of Sheffield Steel Products, he had amassed a significant fortune and been created a baronet in the 1920 Birthday Honours List. His purchase of Fingask Castle from Andrew's grandfather was seen as providing him with the landed respectability he so desperately craved.

Alas, as the British economy fluctuated so did Sir John's wealth, and the aspiring laird soon found himself facing financial ruin. The year was 1923 and, in a bold measure to alleviate his predicament, he decided to sink all that remained of his money into chartering a ship to send cases of Scotch whisky to America, a country in the early throes of Prohibition. Prior to the ship's sailing, Sir John had instructed the captain that no news was good news.

He must have had a premonition because the cargo of Scotch was impounded on arrival by the USA customs authorities. An urgent telegram was sent to Sir John, arriving at Fingask Castle by taxi on 6 February 1924.

Sir John was last seen alive by the taxi-driver who delivered the fateful news. The following day the baronet's lifeless body was discovered by two businessmen whom he had summoned to a meeting at the castle. It was patently clear that on the arrival of the telegram, Sir John had put a gun to his head and shot himself. He was forty-four years old.

Although the Henderson-Stewart baronetcy passed to his son, the castle and estate were sold to cover Sir John's debts. Since then Fingask Castle has had three owners, but as darkness falls it has been a commonplace occurrence for its occupants to hear what sounds like a diesel taxi turning on the gravel sweep and driving off slowly into the night.

15

KEEPING IT IN THE FAMILY

They are not long, the weeping and the laughter,
Love and desire and hate:
I think they have no portion in us after
We pass the gate.

Ernest Dowson, *Vitae Summa Brevis* (1921)

One and a half miles from the ferry terminal at Craignure on the island of Mull is Torosay Castle. Originally a smaller house stood here but it was demolished in 1850 when the eminent Scottish architect David Bryce was employed to build the baronial-style palace that exists there today. In 1865, the Torosay estate was purchased by Arbuthnot Charles Guthrie, the prosperous younger son of a successful banking family, and, on his death, the property passed to his nephew, Murray Guthrie.

By all accounts Murray Guthrie was a renaissance man and it was he who enlisted the services of Sir Robert Lorimer, another great Scottish architect, to create three Italianate terraces and a Statue Walk to connect the castle with its original walled garden. These he decorated with a series of nineteen life-sized limestone statues by the Italian sculptor Antonio Bonazza.

The Statue Walk at Torosay has therefore long been admired

by those fortunate enough to visit Mull, providing a tranquil escape into an island Arcadia. But since the house and grounds were opened to the public in 1975, visitors have often been equally distracted by the stately lady dressed in green who silently steps out in front of them before inexplicably vanishing around a corner of the pathway.

Today, Torosay is owned and occupied by Murray Guthrie's great-grandson, Christopher James, who smiles to himself whenever he hears that the green lady has been seen again. She is, in fact, his great-great-aunt, and he and his wife and children feel entirely comfortable with her presence in and around their home.

The story goes that in 1936, Christopher's great-grandmother Olive Guthrie was seated in her drawing room when her housekeeper rushed in to say that she had just seen Mrs Mary Crawshay, Olive's sister, walking down the drive wearing her characteristic long green cape.

'If you'd told me that Mrs Crawshay was coming to stay, I'd have prepared her room for her and put a hot-water bottle in her bed!' she scolded her mistress crossly.

Olive Guthrie stared at the housekeeper in open amazement. At that precise moment she had just received a telegram informing her that her sister had died.

Mary Crawshay has since settled in happily at Torosay, and is regularly encountered by bemused visitors with no previous knowledge of her history. So far as anyone needs to be concerned, she is, after all, just one of the family.

It may have something to do with islands, but an equally benign apparition is to be found on Orkney at Skaill House on the Breckness Estate at Sandwick. Rising stark and white against the surrounding flat landscape, this classic Orcadian dwelling house was built for a bishop, but after he was ousted in the

Reformation, successive lairds, twelve of them to date, have individually enhanced the property and made it what it is today.

Open to the public between March and September, Skaill House has recently been extensively renovated, and with two self-catering apartments for rent, one upstairs in the house and the other on the ground floor, you might imagine that its owner would want to keep its supernatural residents to himself, but not at all.

If anything, they have become something of an attraction. When guests are woken during the middle of the night by somebody sitting on the corner of their bed, they know that they have nothing to be scared of. It is only Ubby.

In front of Skaill House is Loch Skaill in the middle of which, according to local sources, a reclusive man called Ubby created a man-made island.

Day after day, he rowed his small boat loaded with rocks and stone into the middle of the loch and tipped his cargo overboard until an islet was formed. When it was sufficiently large for him to inhabit, he built a shelter on it and lived there until he died.

Nobody knows exactly when he died, but when the wind whips up and the loch water gets choppy, he was known to come ashore and take refuge in the big house. In recent generations, nobody has ever actually seen his ghost, but his presence in and around the house is widely welcomed.

'Ubby often comes to visit us,' confirms Mary Connolly, who manages Skaill House for the Macrae family. 'He certainly doesn't mean any harm. He just likes us to know that he's here.'

Castles need to have their guardians. There are those that are embedded in the bricks and mortar. Some only reveal themselves when their habitat is threatened, such as in that hilarious film of 1935, *The Ghost Goes West*, in which the resident ghost runs amok when an American millionaire buys his ancestral home and transports it brick by brick across the Atlantic.

The author Nigel Tranter, a great champion of castle restoration, once told me how he had been taken to inspect Inchdrewer Castle in Banffshire. As he was being shown through the door, a gigantic white dog rushed past him from inside the building. Since the castle had been closed for several weeks it was assumed that the animal must have been locked in by accident. Moreover, nobody knew who it belonged to and when a search was made, it was nowhere to be found. Tranter then went on to discover that Inchdrewer Castle was believed to be haunted by the ghost of a lady in a white dress, a member of the Ogilvie family who had once owned the castle. In moments of panic, it seems, she was by some existential power able to transform herself into a large white dog.

There are happy and unhappy hauntings. The less well-known stories, such as that of Mary Crawshay at Torosay, are the outcome of contentment in life and the return of a spirit to where it wants to be. Others, unfortunately, relate to violent incidents, grievances and misfortune. I am not sure whether any of this applies to the unfortunate Helen Gunn of Braemore, but she certainly had every reason to be angry.

It was a haute couture clothes shoot for the newspaper *Scotland on Sunday* that took the fashion designer Chris Clyne to Ackergill Castle, near Wick, in 1989. She was accompanied by two models and the photographer Rob Wilson, and they were the guests of the castle's owners, John and Arlette Bannister.

The setting was superb. Beyond and below the window of the room she was given, Chris could see the North Sea, swelling and restless in Sinclair's Bay, where a P&O ferry was sheltering within canon range. The atmosphere and elegance of the fifteenth-century fortress provided a perfect backdrop for both Chris's casual country dresses and her equally feminine evening gowns. She was delighted, and John and Arlette could not have been more accommodating.

They had made their joint fortune through packaging and had been on the point of buying a building in London when a chance visit to Sutherland brought them to Ackergill. It was love at first sight and within two years they had transformed this crumbling fortress into an immensely successful residential conference venture.

Such places were built to adapt with the times. Over the centuries, Ackergill Tower has constantly had to withstand the conflicts of the eastern Highland clans, and for a time was even garrisoned by Oliver Cromwell. And more than 500 years ago, Helen Gunn of Braemore was imprisoned within its walls by Dugald Keith, her ardent admirer.

A marriage had been arranged between Helen and another suitor, but on the eve of the wedding ceremony, she had been snatched away by Dugald Keith, who removed her to Ackergill. What took place between them within its walls we shall never know, but being determined not to succumb to his advances, Helen chose instead to fling herself from the battlements.

A commemoration stone on the shoreline below marks the spot where she died, but dressed in green she continues to walk the turrets of Ackergill at night, as Chris Clyne was to observe when she looked out of her bedroom window after dinner.

'At first I mistook her for one of my models,' said Chris. 'She was of middle height and slim, and her black hair was loose and hanging across her shoulders. She was standing on her own and gazing into the distance. I was beginning to wonder what on earth she was doing out there at that time of night when she stepped forward and disappeared.

'I didn't know what to think. I leaned out of the window to try and make out where she had gone, but there was no trace of her. What I do vividly remember is that she was wearing this wonderful rich green dress and I was so taken by the colour that I matched it up and used it in my summer collection.'

16

WARLOCKS AND WITCHES

Black Magic is not a myth. It is a totally unscientific and emotional form of magic, but it does get results — of an extremely temporary nature. The recoil upon those who practice it is terrific. It is like looking for an escape of gas with a lighted candle. As far as the search goes, there is little fear of failure!

Aleister Crowley, 'The Worst Man in the World', in the *London Sunday Dispatch*, 2 July 1933

Call them what you will, satanists, necromancers, magicians, princes of darkness, warlocks or witches, they abound in the annals of Scotland's antiquity. Over the seventeenth and eighteenth centuries, over 4,000 souls were accused of all kinds of abominations and put to death for their alleged wicked deeds. A small plaque and serpent fountain on the esplanade of Edinburgh Castle marks where over 300 alone were burned.

In 1736, however, the law changed and under the watchful censorship of the Presbyterian Kirk an accused could only be imprisoned for 'pretended witchcraft'. As one might expect, this ruling was cruelly exploited, and, through lack of education and pure naivety, luckless victims were lured into the trap.

If you disliked your neighbour, or coveted their possessions, the simplest recourse was to out them as a witch. Whether anyone believed you or not, it hardly mattered. Everybody loves to hate a bogeyman. The stigma stuck.

As recently as 1944, Helen Duncan, a Perthshire-born woman, was imprisoned under the 1736 Witchcraft Act for revealing in a séance that a ship had been sunk by the German Navy. Worse still, eleven years after her release she was re-imprisoned for conducting yet another séance.

In this day and age it seems absurd, so much so that a petition was recently presented to the Scottish Parliament demanding she be granted a full pardon which, needless to say, is unlikely to bring much comfort to Helen, since she died over fifty years ago. Perhaps her spirit will feel vindicated, but I do not believe you can make amends for the wrongs of the past by gratifying the current fancies of the living. Yet, having said that, I do believe that Helen Duncan deserves her pardon.

Both black and white witches continue to practise their arts as furtively as they were obliged to in the past, many of them for reasons they are loath to reveal. Whether any of us are aware of it or not, the practice of witchcraft and demonology is not only ubiquitous, but thriving, to some extent encouraged by the phenomenal success of JK Rowling's *Harry Potter* books.

I have a friend, for example, who annually employs a white witch to sweep her home of bad karma. 'It's a precaution,' she says. 'Infestation isn't nearly as threatening as it used to be, but it nevertheless puts my mind at rest.'

In her case it seems to work, but I'm not convinced that it is entirely successful. Necromancy has a vindictive way of clinging to its earthly habitat.

Motorists driving along the B862, their eyes fixated on Loch Ness, barely notice the low-lying one-storey bungalow that crouches on a rise above them.

Yet less than 100 years ago this unprepossessing dwelling with its two surrounding acres of land became notorious as the power-base of the occultist, magician, mountaineer, poet and drug addict Aleister Crowley. During his occupancy, it is said that Boleskine House was surrounded by evil.

So who was this sinister and controversial figure? And why did his presence in this isolated spot make such an impact far beyond the eastern shore of Loch Ness?

Aleister Crowley was born into a wealthy Methodist family in England in 1875, and by all accounts enjoyed an indulgent, reckless childhood, even claiming to have lost his virginity at the age of fourteen. At Cambridge, according to his memoirs, he luxuriated in a voracious sex life with both men and women, and, at one stage, even joined the Plymouth Brethren, although how he reconciled them with his libidinous behaviour is anyone's guess.

His epiphany, however, arrived at the age of twenty-three. Asleep in a hotel in Stockholm, he awoke to a sensation of ghostly terror which simultaneously turned into the purest and holiest of spiritual ecstasy. This somehow persuaded him to enrol with the Hermetic Order of the Golden Dawn, a movement run by the occultist Samuel Liddell Macgregor Mathers, who believed that he was in touch with a group of superhumans known as the Secret Chiefs.

As a community, the Golden Dawn embraced the entire gamut of spiritual knowledge, amalgamating astrology, divination, tarot, numerology and ritual magic, and in addition claimed a spiritual provenance with the Rosicrucian Brotherhood and Kabbalah. Initiated into the order as Brother Perdurabo, Crowley was told by his appointed 'guardian angel' to build an oratory. With his inheritance, he bought Boleskine House, a small eighteenth-century farm building in Inverness-shire. Crowley was then only twenty-four years of age, floppy-haired, strikingly handsome and infinitely more charismatic than the bloated, manic figure that he would later become.

Writing in *The Confessions of Aleister Crowley*, a book published in 1922, he noted:

> The first essential is a house in a more or less secluded situation. There should be a door opening to the north from the room of which you make your oratory. Outside this door, you construct a terrace covered with fine river sand. This ends in a 'lodge' where the spirits may congregate.

Boleskine's owner was determined that his home should become a focal point for magical energies, and although we will never know for certain what took place there, the evidence suggests that Gnostic masses were practised, the model for the orgies so vividly described in Dan Brown's best-selling mystery novel *The Da Vinci Code*. Such goings-on, coupled with the pack of bloodhounds Crowley kept in the kennels, inevitably gave rise to all manner of speculation.

It comes as no surprise therefore to learn that Crowley's coachman rapidly turned to drink, and that, almost immediately after her appointment, his housekeeper packed her bags and fled. When the local butcher called to collect an order and unwittingly interrupted Crowley during a ritual, the latter is said to have scribbled the names of the demons Elerion and Mahakiel on his order. Later that day, while cutting up the meat in his back shop, the unfortunate man somehow managed to slice into one of his arteries. He died on the spot.

Overbearing and conceited, Crowley was expelled from the Order of the Golden Dawn in 1900 and, in the decade that followed, travelled to India, Mexico, and Egypt. This meant that he was more often abroad than at Boleskine, but the rumours of demonic rites persisted. Villagers would allegedly close themselves into their houses at night and prayers would be said whenever he was expected to return.

Boleskine House was sold in 1913, shortly after Crowley was appointed head of the English-speaking branch of the Ordo Templi Orientis, the Order of the Templars of the East, also famous for its unnatural sex rituals. For the duration of the First World War, he based himself in America. On returning to the United Kingdom, however, he was ostracised for having written a series of anti-British articles.

In 1920, Crowley moved to the Mediterranean island of Sicily, where he set up the Abbey of Thelema, but, after accusations of black magic, he was expelled. Never one to give up, he was elected World Head of the Ordo Templi Orientis at the age of fifty. Four years later, he published his seminal work *Magick: In Theory and Practice*. When he died in 1947 at the age of seventy-two, Aleister Crowley had travelled a very long way from Loch Ness. Even so, his name will always be indelibly stamped on the district. When the Led Zeppelin guitarist Jimmy Page purchased Boleskine House in the 1970s, its past associations, he claimed, were a major selling point. In an interview with journalist Steve Pender in 1975, Page revealed that the lure of witchcraft was irresistible.

'I don't really want to go on about my personal beliefs or my involvement in magic,' he explained. 'I'm not interested in turning anybody on to anything that I'm turned on to . . . if people want to find things, they find them themselves. I'm a firm believer in that.'

Although Aleister Crowley's spectre has long since dimmed, it did undergo a modest revival in the 1960s when his face was featured on the album sleeve of the Beatles' *Sergeant Pepper's Lonely Hearts Club Band*. Possibly because of this, he achieved a certain celebrity status among the hippy community, and when Neil Oram's twenty-four-hour long play about a mystic, *The Warp*, featured on the Edinburgh Fringe in 1980, strange goings-on were re-enacted on the banks of Loch Ness.

Occultism, as I observed earlier, is far from being a dormant phenomenon. With the decline of the orthodox churches, paganism is on the rise again throughout America and western Europe. Although practices and beliefs may be, by definition, diverse, and for the most part not to be taken too seriously, covens and sects are currently more active than they have been for centuries. Moreover, they are to be found in the most unexpected places.

Jan Spalding was not intentionally drawn towards sorcery, but in her mid-thirties she found herself still a spinster and living with her widowed mother in the main street of a small village in Stirlingshire. Her father had died, or at least that was the understanding. He had, in fact, eloped with an accountant's daughter half his age, and Jan and her mother Pru chose not to talk about it.

And to some extent that was why they had moved to live in Stirlingshire, where they knew nobody and nobody knew them. It was a fresh start, and Jan, with her academic qualifications, was easily able to secure a teaching post at the local preparatory school.

More importantly, she loved the job and only occasionally yearned for the social distractions of a big city. The village, meanwhile, was pretty, and the terraced cottage which she and her mother occupied was warm and extremely comfortable.

But Jan was also only too well aware that her life was passing her by. Her looks, she suspected, were fading; wrinkles were proliferating around her eyes. Despite attempts to diet, she was steadily putting on weight.

And it was with this in mind that she decided to join a leisure complex that had just opened up in a not too distant location, and it was here that she met up with and befriended Rachel and Alice. The three women were much of an age and soon became inseparable, to the extent that one evening, after a sweat in the leisure club sauna, Rachel and Alice invited Jan to join their coven.

At first she thought they must be joking. However, it soon became apparent that they were in deadly earnest.

Oh why not? she decided, and, the following Saturday, the three of them set off on their bicycles and into the Trossachs for what she was told would be an induction ritual. This induction ritual, much to her mild embarrassment, involved swimming naked in a loch by moonlight, and encircling a large oak tree while the two other women joined hands and chanted incantations. Fortunately for them, it was in the height of summer and the midges had momentarily retreated.

'From now on we share our powers,' announced Rachel and Alice, handing over several books on pagan ritual and a modern witchcraft guide. Jan blushed as she zipped up her anorak. She nevertheless felt secretly rather proud of herself.

From then on, the excursions took place every month, along with weekly visits to the health club. Pru, Jan's mother, remained happily at home in front of her television set, and, kindly soul that she was, never asked where her daughter had been, no doubt assuming that were it of any importance she would be told.

Mother and daughter were content enough, but that was to end abruptly when Norman Lovet arrived in the district. Norman was a widower of sixty who had taken early retirement to write a novel. For this purpose, he had rented a small former shooting bothy and, despite insisting that he was in search of solitude, his eye was one day caught by the glimpse of a woman buying milk from the village shop. On further investigation, he was to learn that she was Miss Jan Spalding, a teacher at the village school. The designation 'Miss' sent a shiver of anticipation up his spine.

To be fair, Norman had been faithful to his late wife for over thirty years, only once dallying with an air hostess on a business trip to Singapore. Prior to his marriage, however, he had been considered a bit of a catch and notched up an impressive portfolio of conquests before succumbing to the charms and substantial bank balance of his employer's daughter.

That, of course, was the problem. Throughout his career Norman, his marital duties preoccupying every minute of his spare time, had been kept far too busy to philander. Now that his wife was gone – taken by breast cancer at the age of fifty – he had all the time in the world to feel sorry for himself, and, despite the creative urges which drove him to spend hours of torment in front of a word processor, he was bored.

And that was when the trouble began. On the pretext of delivering a package to the wrong address, Norman had one afternoon called upon Mrs Pru Spalding in the hope of encountering her daughter. Jan was not in at the time, but Pru had made Norman suitably welcome. There followed flowers, and in gratitude Pru invited him to Sunday tea to meet Jan. Having been formally introduced, the courting commenced in earnest, with Norman entirely oblivious to the fact that Jan was not even remotely interested in him.

It was most unfortunate. He had never previously been spurned by the opposite sex, and Norman's persistence soon became an embarrassment. As the days passed, it was inevitable that Rachel and Alice should be drawn into the fiasco.

Sensing their friend's growing irritation with the constant phone calls and the notes of endearment that were pushed under her front door almost every other night, they proposed that something be done about it.

'Why don't we cast a spell over him?' suggested Rachel. 'I'm sure we can look up some ancient curse to sort him out. There must be something we can do. His sort have been around for centuries.'

That weekend, once again exploring the Trossachs, the three women unloaded their picnic and, consulting a book of spells, set about the bewitching of Norman Lovet.

'In the night and in this hour, we call upon the ancient powers. Bring them to we sisters three. A eunuch will he henceforth be.'

None of them took any of this particularly seriously, and when they had finished chanting aloud under the night sky, they all three rolled around on the ground convulsed in laughter. 'That'll teach him,' cried out Alice. 'That'll teach him to meddle with the Trossach witches.'

The following day was a Monday, and Jan set off bright and early for school as usual. On her way, she glanced over towards the bothy and experienced just a slight twinge of guilt. There was no sign of movement, so she relaxed. However, later that morning she received a call from her mother, who sounded distraught.

'I thought you should know about poor Norman,' said Pru in a voice charged with emotion.

'What's happened, Mum?' said Jan with a mounting feeling of dread.

'It's just too terrible to talk about,' said Pru. 'It's Norman, the poor man. He was crossing Farmer MacEwan's field yesterday afternoon, you know the one we've all been warned to avoid, and he got trampled by that great brute of a bull. It's just too dreadful. I've seen the district nurse and she says he'll never be able to father children!'

17

THE LANDSCAPE OVER THE FIREPLACE

A house is never still in darkness to those who listen intently; there is a whispering in distant chambers, an unearthly hand presses the snib of the window, the latch rises. Ghosts were created when the first man awoke in the night.

JM Barrie, *The Little Minister* (1891)

The massive oil painting had hung in its heavy gilt frame over Great-aunt Alison's fireplace for as long as Sandra could remember. She had never paid much attention to it when she was a child, but now that the old lady was dead, Sandra had come to take stock of the gloomy Victorian house in Woodside, on the outskirts of Aberdeen. For such a prominently placed picture, it appeared strikingly modern amid its period surroundings of flock wallpaper, faded chintz and wilted pot plants. Only its frame kept faith with the early twentieth-century decor.

A sense of guilt gripped Sandra Pottinger as she and her great-aunt's executor, a gauche young lawyer in a striped suit, explored the print-hung corridors and poked about among the dusty

135

rooms, several of which seemed not to have seen the light of day for years. A pang of guilt enveloped her. Over the past ten years she had been far too busy with her own life bringing up her children and making ends meet to maintain contact with the old lady. At least, that was her excuse. Now it was too late. Sandra knew she should have made more of an effort over Great-aunt Alison. She had been the last of that generation, and as her nearest relative, all of this, the house and its contents, now belonged to Sandra. Knowing this simply enhanced the realisation that she had hardly known her grandmother's younger sister.

As she appraised the bulky Victorian wood furniture, the porcelain bric-a-brac, threadbare rugs and heavy curtain drapes, it seemed that all that she and the lawyer could think about was how much was everything worth. How horrible to think that once you are gone, that is all there is to it; an entire existence, relegated to an auction saleroom to generate cash.

By now, Sandra's conscience was really playing up. Great-aunt Alison had barely been cremated and here they were, these virtual strangers behaving like predatory vultures, evaluating how much the house and its treasures would fetch; the treasures of an old lady's entire lifetime; treasures Sandra had never expected to inherit.

Alison Bradie was in her nineties when she died, and little if any contact had been maintained with her since the death of Sandra's mother fourteen years earlier. There had been the generous gift of some silver when Sandra married, a nuisance to keep clean but nonetheless welcome. Being reluctant to travel, Great-aunt Alison had not attended the wedding. Christmas cards had nevertheless been exchanged annually, and when the children were born, Sandra had sent photographs.

Of course, Sandra had known the house well when she herself was a child, but in all innocence had never asked any of the questions she should have about Great-aunt Alison. All she knew about her was that she had never married, a stigma for her parents' generation that you did not talk about; that in her middle age Great-aunt Alison had worked as a housekeeper for a wealthy bachelor who, when he died, had left her his house with a small private income. Perhaps Sandra was imagining it, but she was sure that there had been some sort of mystery about Great-aunt Alison's early life. It had never been mentioned by the family, although Alison and her sister, Sandra's grandmother, had remained close until the latter's death.

When Sandra's parents moved to live in the south of England, it became too much of an excursion for them to return regularly to Aberdeen, and Sandra had no recollection of Great-aunt Alison ever visiting them in Surrey. As the years flew past, she had almost forgotten that Alison existed, that is until the solicitor's letter arrived. Her death had come out of the blue, but as it transpired, proved a timely blessing.

There were school fees and the mortgage to pay. With her husband Paul being passed over for advancement in the sports promotion agency where he worked, every little helped.

As Sandra continued her inspection of the house, she once more succumbed to a great well of regret. Great-aunt Alison had certainly lived to a good age; she had had a good innings, as people say when they can think of nothing else.

But that did not make Sandra feel any better. Great-aunt Alison was the last link with her own mother's past. Despite her inheritance, and the money it brought her, Sandra was only too aware that this was somebody she felt she had never really known, and would never now have the opportunity to know. How selfish we are when we are young, she murmured under her breath as the thoughts accumulated.

It appeared that, latterly, Great-aunt Alison had occupied only a bedroom on the first floor, and the stone-flagged kitchen with its ancient Aga in the basement. The public rooms were closed up.

Although fiercely independent, Alison Bradie had asked neither family nor friends for help. Towards the end there had been day visitors who kept her fed and watered and to some extent cleaned the rooms. Sandra's first instinct on entering through the front porch had been to throw open the shutters and windows to allow fresh air to circulate. It was a bright autumn day with a brisk North Sea off-shore breeze. As Sandra stood on her own in the drawing room, a shaft of yellow sunlight fell on the oil painting hanging over the fireplace and she was struck by its beauty. She had never before rated Scottish landscapes. They were generally too stark and overpowering, with lots of orange cattle dotted about. But this one was exceptional. It was hypnotic.

Decades of smoke from the open fireplace had coated its surface, but the colours still shone through. Sandra could clearly make out a range of hills overhung with racing rainclouds. In the foreground was a wisp of smoke climbing from the chimney of a tiny dwelling place on the shores of a silver loch. In an adjacent field were two figures seemingly absorbed in chopping wood. Tucked into the fold of a hill was a small church, encroached upon by a graveyard. The detail was fantastic, thought Sandra, searching for a signature or clue as to the artist's identity.

All she could make out was the date – 1938 – and an indecipherable squiggle. No clue was given as to the location. Sandra's thoughts were racing ahead of her when they were interrupted by the arrival of Alison's lawyer carrying the urn with her ashes. Ignoring this, Sandra asked him if he knew anything about the painting.

'You'll find out when it is valued for probate,' he informed her, placing the urn on a side table. 'Probably fetch you a couple of grand in the auction rooms.'

As he spoke, a Georgian carriage clock perched prominently on the mantelpiece overturned and crashed to the floor, the glass cracking. 'That's a shame,' he continued briskly. 'That would have been worth a few bob.'

Sandra stared at him. 'Did you know my great-aunt?' she asked.

'Only met her once,' he replied. 'Old McKillop, the senior partner, looked after her affairs. We'd all expected him to pack it in when he hit seventy, but he just went on and on and on until the Almighty gathered him in January. What a way to go! He fell off his bike at a protest meeting to stop that American building a golf course on Balmeddie Beach. A great golfer, was Old McKillop, but he didn't want his beloved environment to be buggered up.'

'Balmeddie Beach? Is that somewhere I could scatter my great-aunt's ashes?' asked Sandra on impulse.

'No chance,' came the response. 'Miss Bradie was very specific about that in her will. She wanted them to go into the sea somewhere called Loch Buie. I think it's on Mull.'

Sandra looked appalled. 'How on earth am I expected to do that?' she gasped. 'I don't even know where Mull is, let alone Loch Buie.'

The young lawyer smiled. 'That's your problem, Mrs Pottinger,' he said, gesturing towards the urn. 'I'd best get back to the office.'

When Paul telephoned Sandra that evening, she told him about Great-aunt Alison's last wishes.

'I wouldn't bother, if I were you,' he said. 'She's long past caring about that now.'

Sandra was inclined to agree, but her conscience still pricked her with a gnawing doubt that was unlikely to be dispersed when she decided to stay overnight in the old house. The least she could do was consult the touring map in the glove pocket of her hire car. And there it was. Loch Buie was situated on the south coast of the island of Mull, fourteen miles from the ferry terminal at Craignure.

'Sorry, Great-aunt Alison,' muttered Sandra under her breath as she climbed into bed. 'You'll have to make do with Balmeddie.'

The night fell silent, but towards daybreak Sandra awoke to a persistent rattling noise coming from downstairs. At first she tried to ignore it, but the sound merely increased in volume. Finally she went to investigate and, wrapping herself in a dressing gown, descended the staircase. The sounds were coming from the drawing room, but stopped when she entered and switched on the lights.

The first thing she noticed was that the funeral urn had been moved to the fireplace. She could have sworn it had been on the side table where the lawyer had left it, but it was now pressed up against the fire guard, where the clock had fallen. Convinced her mind was playing tricks on her, Sandra flicked the light switch inside the door, but the over-light above the oil painting remained on. That was odd, she thought to herself. There must be another switch but, search as she did, she was unable to locate it. There were no connections on either side of the fireplace. Nor could she see plugs on the skirting board.

That was very odd. Moreover, she could not remember the over-light having been on before, and once again she found herself staring at the painting. It was certainly striking, she confirmed to herself, and this time she noticed that there was something that looked like lettering under the paintwork in the left-hand corner. Removing a handkerchief from her pocket, she dampened the fabric with her tongue and rubbed the surface. As she continued to rub, the dirt slowly lifted away and, much to her amazement, the words 'Loch Buie' were revealed.

It was at that moment she decided that despite the inconvenience, she would take Great-aunt Alison's ashes to Loch Buie.

When she returned to bed, the house became silent and Sandra fell into a deep sleep in which she dreamed of a woman in her early twenties and a man of around the same age. They were laughing together as they cast fishing lines over the side of a small boat floating on a loch surrounded by high hills. The following morning, the overwhelming sense of happiness created by the dream filled Sandra with a sensation of great contentment.

That morning, having secured all of the doors and windows, Sandra packed her suitcase, loaded Great-aunt Alison's ashes into the boot of the car, and set off to drive west, bypassing Inverness, to travel south and south-west again towards Argyllshire and the sea port of Oban. It was midday by the time she arrived at the ferry terminal, but she was just in time to book the car onto the CalMac. At Craignure, she asked for directions to Loch Buie and set off to follow the signs to Fionnphort, turning south onto one of the narrowest and windiest tracks she had ever seen.

When eventually she arrived at the village of Lochbuie, on the curve of Loch Buie, it was mid-afternoon. Rounding a corner, she pulled over beside the loch to inspect the picturesque little church, which she recognised instantly. It was the church in the oil painting. At the door stood an elderly woman, her hair tucked up into a woollen bonnet, her shoulders wrapped in a plaid shawl.

'You'll be the one with Alison Bradie's ashes,' she said in a matter-of-fact manner.

Sandra stared at the stranger in astonishment. 'How can you possibly know that?' she gasped.

The woman's face cracked in a smile. 'I saw in the newspaper she'd gone. They called me from Craignure to tell me you were on your way.'

People on islands are still like that, thought Sandra. She remembered having told the ferry master the purpose of her visit. 'But who are you?' she exclaimed, bewildered.

'Let me show you,' said the woman gently. Taking Sandra's hand, she led her round the side of the church to a simple commemorative stone. On it was carved: 'Rhuaridh Maclean. Painter, sculptor and lobster fisherman. 1912–1939. Lost at Sea.'

'Rhuaridh was my oldest brother,' she explained. 'I am Norma Maclean. Alison was betrothed to Rhuaridh, but my father did his utmost to prevent them from marrying because he didn't approve of the way Rhuaridh earned his living.

'Besides, he said Alison was too young. Such nonsense. She was nineteen, and her parents liked Rhuaridh, so there was not much my parents could do about it.

'And it was not as if Rhuaridh didn't have his own money. He sold a lot of his paintings. He was very successful – he even exhibited at the Royal Scottish Academy in Edinburgh. So they decided to come here to a croft on the Moy estate in search of the simple life. Mull's a great place to live if you're an artist . . .' She paused. 'But you must be one of the family,' she said as an afterthought.

'Her great-niece,' said Sandra. 'Alison left me her house in Aberdeen.'

Norma nodded. 'My brother's house,' she said.

'How do you mean? I thought Great-aunt Alison worked there as the owner's housekeeper?'

'That was Lachlan, my other brother,' replied Norma. 'Like me, he wasn't that keen on marriage, was Lachlan, especially when he saw how my father treated our mother and our brother. When Rhuaridh died, Lachlan offered Alison a home. I think that he'd always had a thing for her, but he'd never have done anything about it. That was Lachlan.

'She couldn't stay here on Mull, of course. Or rather, she wouldn't stay here. There was too much sorrow. Lachlan and Alison always liked each other, but there was no way he would have married her and nor would she have wanted to marry him.

'So the only way for it to be respectable in those days was for her to be his housekeeper and keep to her own quarters. They were together for almost half a century. She looked after him well.'

'But what happened to Rhuaridh?'

Norma Maclean gave off a deep, weary sigh and gazed across Loch Buie towards the Firth of Lorne. 'One day Rhuaridh just went off in his little motor boat and he never returned. Upturned by the tide off Carsaig Bay, they said. His body should have washed up on the shore near Malcolm's Point, but it was never found. Alison was devastated. She never recovered from her loss. It broke her heart. That's why she left. That's why all these long years later she needs to return.'

Something still did not make sense. 'How is it that you're here?' asked Sandra. 'It's just so strange.'

'I needed to escape from Aberdeen too.' Her voice betrayed her emotion. 'I had been seeing a local boy and found myself pregnant. My brothers and I were close. I was sixteen at the time and when we lost Rhuaridh, Lachlan took over Alison's tenancy of the croft for me. They were good men, my brothers Lachlan and Rhuaridh. Nobody knew me here. I had a fatherless child to bring up and with my mother dead, my father wanted nothing to do with me. So I came here. I've moved house on the island twice since, but never more than a mile.'

Their eyes met with a mutual understanding. 'I think Alison would have wanted us both to be here for her today,' said Sandra. 'Shall we?'

Together the two women followed the stoney path toward the water's edge. Removing the cap of the urn, Sandra shook the white powder briskly onto the wind and the two women watched as it dispersed like icing sugar over the restless expanse of water in front of them.

'She'll be happy again,' said Sandra.

'They'll both be happy again,' her companion corrected her.

18

THE COLD HEARTH

Good things of day begin to droop and drowse,
Whiles night's black agents to their preys do rouse.

William Shakespeare, *Macbeth*, 3.3 (*c* 1603–07)

On the fashionable south side of Glasgow, Will and Janice Laidlaw were thrilled when their offer for a tenement flat in Pollokshaws was accepted. Janice had always longed for a place of her own to redecorate to her own inimitable taste, and from the moment they moved in had set about re-traditionalising the interiors.

First of all there was the kitchen, followed by the bedrooms and living room. The latter was a big problem as its only decorative feature was a small, nondescript gas fire, whereas Janice was determined to have a spacious open hearth surmounted by an imposing mantelpiece. Fortunately, Will was a bit of a genius when it came to do-it-yourself and recycling, and he was prepared to go to any length to please his best beloved.

That first winter, they made do, but as soon as the clocks went forward at the end of March, Will announced he was planning to entirely rebuild the fireplace. 'Don't worry, it won't cost us anything. I found a whole stack of stone lying unused in an old abandoned yard down the road. If nobody wants it, we might as well make the best of it.'

Janice was thrilled. As a van driver for the council, it was a relatively easy task for Will to pick up the necessary materials on his travels and soon afterwards large slabs of stone began to appear on the tenement stair. While this was going on, Janice retreated into the kitchen, leaving her husband and his pal to get on with the work.

It took several weeks and created a lot of noise and clouds of dust which filled the entire building like a sandstorm, but when the work was completed Janice was thrilled at the result. It was as if the entire wall of the sitting room had been replaced. Instead of the small, ugly stove there now stood the most magnificent opening of pink and white-streaked marble surmounted by a black marble mantelshelf, under which Will had inserted a flueless living flame fire. It was a marvel. 'It makes me feel like royalty,' Janice told Will.

Or at least that was her first reaction. Throughout the summer months she would proudly show it off to friends who dropped in for a visit, but after a certain amount of time had passed, it occurred to her that there was always something missing in their response. Nobody was ever as enthusiastic as she had expected them to be. They were polite, yes, but that was all.

And on further reflection she realised why. Despite the flame being turned on to its fullest extent, the room always remained inexplicably chilly. It was as if there were a permanent north wind hovering over the hearth. As autumn moved towards winter, the temperature continued to drop. Often Janice felt that it was con-siderably warmer outside in the street.

'Why does the fire give off so little heat?' she chided Will one day, shivering as she increased the flame. Outside the sun was shining, but inside the Laidlaws' sitting room it remained as cold as the interior of their refrigerator.

Will too was puzzled. 'Perhaps it's the marble,' he said. 'Marble is supposed to keep things cool, isn't it? That's why they use it in all those eastern palaces and places like Dubai.'

'In a warm climate, but not one like this,' Janice responded. 'It's gae bitter here.'

As December approached, the situation did not improve. Eventually, Will was obliged to invest in a portable calor gas heater. Then one morning, Janice, who had been examining the fire surround, asked Will where the stone had come from.

'Look,' she pointed out. 'There are some words carved into the edge of this slab here.'

Will had not noticed these markings before and now studied them closely. They ran along a section of the fireplace surround and he could just make out the lettering, *Dearly Beloved.* He shook his head.

'Well, I did tell you that somebody had abandoned this stuff,' he said. 'We did get it for free.'

Janice shook her head. 'That's all fine and dandy, but where did it come from? That's what I'd like to know. And what does it mean, *Dearly Beloved?* I hope it's not masonic.'

'Would it help if I showed you where I got it?' Will volunteered, recognising her irritation.

That afternoon, he took her to the abandoned yard where he had helped himself to the stone. It had seemed harmless enough at the time. He recalled a boarded-up shed and the large notice board advertising the site for sale. He knew exactly where it was, but when they arrived he discovered that the shed had been dismantled. In its place stood a property show-room with a sign announcing that the site was in the process of being developed into luxury apartments. Behind a desk sat an earnest young man

147

in a suit who looked up eagerly as they entered. 'Are you interested in buying?' he asked hopefully.

Janice shook her head. 'No,' she said. 'We were just wondering what this place was before?'

The salesman looked disappointed, but did not wish to appear unhelpful. 'Blythe & Thompson, Monumental Masons,' he told them. 'They went into administration and we bought the land. Nobody can afford tombstones nowadays.'

Janice looked at Will in horror. 'You mean to say . . . ?' Her voice trailed off as the reality of the marble's provenance dawned on her. Glaring at her husband, she turned on her heels and headed back to the van, muttering under her breath.

'Would you like a prospectus?' the young man called after her.

Soon afterwards, a For Sale sign appeared on the Laidlaws' flat in Pollokshaws. Will and Janice now live in a new-build apartment in Govan.

19

THE GREAT HECTOR

Hard, swift intelligence is so apt to hate and wish to
cast aside what it cannot comprehend.

Annie S. Swan, *The Land I Love* (1936)

Hebridean islanders have a reputation for being tuned into the
nonconformity of the elements. With the exception of the advent
of electricity, the telephone, motor cars and air transport, nothing
much has changed since the dawn of time on the far-flung land
masses of the Small Isles, Harris and Lewis or the Uists. In this
landscape of the moon, an acceptance of the supernatural is
ingrained in the mindset of the Gael. From the sea come sealmen
and sea monsters; selkies and water horses cavort in inland
lochans; folk disappear into the peaty moorland without a trace;
inexplicable lights are seen dancing in the back of beyond.

Overhead, there are the birds of the sky – the eagle, the raven,
the capercaillie and the elusive corncrake. On the land, there are
the red deer.

Nature is a cruel taskmaster. In the raw reality of death and
rebirth, the interaction between man and beast becomes a pitiless challenge. For the red deer to regenerate, they have first to
be reduced, and to this end exists a competitive breed who live

for the chase, intent on pitting the skills of mankind against the instincts of the beast. The key stalking months are from August until October, and the annual cull quotas laid down in law by the Red Deer Commission are expected to be met.

Thus, the landed estates of these islands have earned an unequalled reputation across the centuries for the quality of their sporting trophies. No trees occupy a deer forest, only hostile expanses of scrub and peat. And as a result, some of the finest herds to be found anywhere in the world inhabit the gullies and straths of this often inaccessible landscape, providing an unequalled challenge to the sporting gun.

Morrison Drummond, a financial analyst in the City of London, was one such sporting gun. Since his uncle had given him a shotgun on his eighteenth birthday, Morrison had become obsessed with shooting and stalking, despite living in Essex; perhaps it had something to do with the sedentary nature of his work.

And it was only to be expected that as soon as he was financially established, he should join a syndicate, which, for seven glorious days in late autumn, rented a furnished stalking lodge on the north-west coast of Lewis. Here, under the tuition of Lachlan Mackenzie, the head stalker, Morrison and his three equally virile syndicate colleagues were able to happily indulge their macho appetites and, more importantly, hunt the deer.

It was not so much that Morrison enjoyed killing wild animals: it was the challenge it presented, he told himself, coupled with the exercise and the fresh air, all of this being in such marked contrast to his chosen desk-bound vocation of making money. On these Hebridean islands, so he had been told, existed the last truly wild animals on earth. As wild as wild can possibly be. Although colour blind, a deer can sense the approach of a human being at a distance of ten miles. If anyone manages to come within two miles of one, it becomes a major triumph. This is man pitted against nature in its rawest reality.

There is also the extreme physical challenge of crossing this godforsaken landscape of sodden umber-coloured peat and springy, scratchy heather. However, nothing compares with the thrill of reaching a summit and the sense of wonderment engendered by an uninterrupted vista of lochans, gorges, hills with a distant ocean slicing into the sky. It is at such moments that everything in God's plan falls into place.

And it was on just such an occasion that through his spyglass Morrison caught sight of the Great Hector. Raised high on a plateau, with a canyon of rock and rivulets between them, stood the noble beast, a shaft of sunlight spotlighting his royal crown of antlers.

'Look! Look there!' Morrison whispered audibly to Lachlan. 'What a beauty!'

The stalker raised his telescope and smiled benignly. 'That'll be the Great Hector,' he said softly, with a knowing look. 'But he's long gone.'

Sure enough, when Morrison turned to look again, all he saw was an empty hillside. 'He will have seen the Uists,' said Mackenzie. It was not his practice to indulge those who employed him with his innermost thoughts.

That night as Morrison Drummond slept, he had a vivid dream in which he came across the Great Hector sheltering with a herd of hinds in a deep gully. The wind was blasting through the bleak scrub as mountain burns frothed white in spate. As the sky darkened, Morrison saw himself raise his gun, at which point the Great Hector turned his fine head directly towards him and let out an almighty roar.

The force of the roar deafened the wind. Morrison awoke in a cold sweat.

Sustained by a filling breakfast, Morrison and Lachlan Mackenzie set off to climb Ben Bholly the following morning. It was a steep ascent, but the dry weather held until they were over the top. Far below, they could make out the ragged coastline and ocean. Indeed, had the rapidly changing visibility allowed, they might even have been able to identify Rockall or the dots of the archipelago of St Kilda, far out into the Atlantic.

For a while, it looked as if it would be yet another one of those energetic, demanding days on the hill, with spurts of repetitive, all-enveloping showers of rain punctuated by blasts of hot sun. Alternately soaked and scorched, Morrison and Lachlan continued their pursuit with intermittent sightings. As the afternoon drew on, the weather closed in.

To this day, neither Morrison Dummond nor Lachlan Mackenzie can say for certain what happened next. Mackenzie, whose knowledge of this terrain was inherited from his father and grandfather before him, insists that Morrison had, against his explicit instructions, wandered off. Morrison is adamant that Lachlan abandoned him. 'That simply would not happen,' Lachlan argues in his defence, and everyone who knows him concurs.

'Lachlan Mackenzie is far too professional a stalker to allow anyone in his charge to stray off by themselves, no matter how preoccupied he might be,' I was told by the owner of the lodge.

'It's the stalker's charter to look after his guns,' Lachlan protests angrily whenever the subject of Morrison Drummond is raised.

However, Lachlan is also only too well aware that what occurred on that wet afternoon in August was totally beyond his control.

Bent low so as not to be seen against the hillside, Morrison was following Lachlan on a steep downward path when he noticed movement on the far side of the gully. It was a handsome stag with several hinds. Morrison's knee-jerk reaction had been to fall to the ground and to signal to Lachlan who, as it transpired, was nowhere to be seen.

Regardless, Morrison unslung his rifle, checked the distance, and lined up a shot on the stag in preparation for a clean kill. As he did so, he recalls the rain became a torrent and a sickly, sticky mist began to rise from the heather beneath him. To make himself more comfortable, he rolled over slightly and was on the point of squeezing the trigger when there was a surge of movement from under his thighs and everything around him collapsed. Helpless, he found himself tumbling over and over, down a long, steep, agonising slope, and landing with a thud on a pebbly foreshore at the edge of the sea.

Unable to stabilise itself, Morrison hit the shingle with a sickening thud. A searing pain surged through his femur and he realised that he must have broken his left leg. Petrified, he cried out for help, but heard no sound other than the swishing and shifting of rain, and the hush of the waves.

Then, to his astonishment, his attention was caught by the movement of several hundred deer. To his utter amazement, he saw that leading them was the Great Hector, and they were following him impassively, like lemmings, into the water, where they vanished out of sight. As a spectacle it was both breathtaking and incredible. Morrison had never seen or heard of anything like it ever before. As soon as the last of the herd had nimbly passed below the waves, everything fell very quiet.

With admirable presence of mind Morrison remembered he had two signal flares in his jacket pocket and, having extracted them, fired them into the sky. The burst of red smoke exploded high above, throwing a rosy sheen over his surroundings, but there was no sign of the deer, only the tide.

An hour later, a motor vessel arrived and Morrison was lifted on board. He was taken to the hospital in Stornoway and released, with his leg in plaster, later that night. Still entirely baffled by what had occurred, he determined to give up stalking in favour of some alternative, non-blood sport pastime such as golf or tennis. 'It was an omen,' he informed his friends.

'I was nurtured in my mother's womb with tales of the Great Hector,' said Lachlan Mackenzie when I joined him for a dram at McNeill's Pub in Stornoway. 'Both my father and my grandfather spoke of him, though neither clapped eyes on the brute. These city folk, you know, they come here with their fancy tailored tweeds and their pricey guns, and they think they know it all. It does no harm to give them a jolt now and then.'

Yes, but did Lachlan Mackenzie seriously believe in a ghostly herd of deer led by a phantom stag?

He tapped the side of his nose, swallowed his dram, and winked. 'He'll be far away on the Uists by now,' he said.

20

THE DARK LORD

I've heard my rev'rend grannie say,
In lanely glens ye like to stray;
Or where auld ruin'd castles grey
Nod to the moon,
Ye fright the nightly wand'rer's way,
Wi' eldritch croon.

Robert Burns, 'Address to the De'il' (1785)

Anecdotes about phantom animals – rogue dogs, wolves, inexplicable footprints in the snow – occur throughout Scottish folklore. In most cases there is a perfectly logical explanation. Some of the tales relate directly to animals which have escaped from zoos; others to an Act of Parliament passed in 1976.

The Dangerous Wild Animals Act was introduced to control the number of exotic pets being kept in the United Kingdom, but to some extent it backfired as several owners simply released their pets into the wild. This was the explanation given back then for the numerous sightings of large cats roaming the countryside. Whether or not any them have survived, or succeeded in breeding, remains undetermined, but their continuing metaphysical presence in the landscape cannot be denied.

Galloway Forest Park, the vast area of woodland that covers the 250 square miles where Dumfriesshire spills into the roof of Galloway, is a favourite retreat for walkers, cyclists and lovers of the great outdoors. It was this indeed that brought Andy Gallagher and Donald Drummond, two young friends from Ayr, to the Forestry Commission campsite a couple of miles from Loch Trool.

Both in their early twenties, they had already explored most of the Lake District and Southern Uplands, but this particular corner of Dumfries and Galloway, despite it being situated virtually on their doorstep, was so far unknown to them. Having ascended Glen Trool to inspect Bruce's Stone, they turned off the main road and soon afterwards found their way down a plunging track towards Loch Dee, where they threw off their clothes to swim off one of the pebbly beaches before spending their first night in sleeping bags at the White Laggan Bothy.

With long days of fixed blue sky and an oven-hot sun, the weather could not have been more glorious. Although equipped with jerseys, lycra shorts, open-face plastic helmets, and knee and elbow protection, such bare skin as was exposed rapidly turned nut-brown. Evenings brought the inevitable curse of the midge, but even this was bearable with sausages cooked over a fire of twigs and a few cans of lager. Their sleeping bags unrolled on the edge of a forest enclosure in close proximity to the River Cree, they passed their second night together in perfect harmony. The pressures of the outside world faded far from sight. 'I could live like this forever,' confided Andy as the night closed in.

After the day's exertions, both fell asleep the moment they closed their eyes. Usually, they would have remained unconscious until sunrise but on this particular night they awoke simultaneously.

'There's something over there,' whispered Donald urgently, peering into the gloom. A rustling sound resonated in the long grass on the far side of the clearing, and through the half-light they could make out movement.

'It'll be a deer,' said Andy calmly.

'No, I don't think so,' replied Donald. 'I think it's more like a large cat.'

He turned on his torch and pointed it in the direction of the sounds. For a fleeting couple of seconds, they both saw it; what appeared to be a large black cat, a very large black cat. In an instant they were out of their sleeping bags and although scantily clad, took cover in the undergrowth behind them. After that, there was a silence followed by the sounds of tugging and tearing, and clank of metal as tin cups and a kettle were turned over. Then more silence.

For a full half-hour, neither Andy nor Donald spoke. With no wind, the night air was unnaturally still and heavy. Finally, Andy took the initiative. 'Do you still have the torch?' he asked Donald.

Donald handed it to him. 'What do you think we should do?' he said hesitantly.

'We could just sit here until the sun comes up, but I think that whatever it was would have come for us by now if it was going to,' suggested Andy. 'Thank the Lord, it's already starting to get light.'

Sure enough, in less than an hour a pale sun was gradually caressing the scenery with a pastel wash. Emerging from the prickly undergrowth, the friends looked nervously about them.

'All clear,' said Andy, then groaned. 'Damn! Look what the bastard's done to our kit!'

Across the clearing were signs of devastation. Andy's sleeping bag had been ripped to pieces and their rucksacks plundered, the contents scattered all over the place. 'I reckon we had a bloody lucky escape,' said Donald. 'Thank God the bikes are OK.'

At the Clatteringshaws Visitor Centre, the ranger listened sympathetically to their story. 'Must have escaped from a zoo,' he concluded, shrugging his shoulders. 'I've heard about big cats being seen on Speyside and around Dundee, but never around here.'

'Well, we know what we saw,' said Donald. 'It was as big as a lynx or a puma.'

The ranger smiled and made a note in his diary. 'I'll keep a look out for it,' he said. 'At least it didn't attack you. If it had, we'd have beeen obliged to shoot it.'

That was reassuring, thought Donald. 'What about our things?' he bemoaned. 'My rucksack was brand new!'

The ranger shook his head. 'You could try your insurance, if you have any, but I'd change your story if I were you. Giant cats are a wee bit Walt Disney. They'll probably think you're trying it on.'

Having replaced their damaged belongings, and restocked their food provisions, Andy and Donald set off undeterred, this time wheeling their bikes alongside the shore of the Black Loch to cross the Tenderghie Burn upstream to explore the waterfall. Once more, it was a day to remember as they threw off their shorts and vests to plunge into the icy torrent. That night they stretched out under the stars, orchestrated by the sound of the Grey Mare's Tail Burn splashing nearby.

'Perhaps we should have returned to the campsite,' reflected Donald as he opened a can of lager.

'Nonsense,' replied Andy. 'It's so much better being here. That's what we came for, isn't it, to get away from it all?'

Donald nodded in agreement. In a week's time he would be back at his office desk, wearing a suit and tie. He should make the best of it.

As the light faded around them, they lay talking to one another in their sleeping bags until eventually they fell sleep. Yet again, it was in the early hours that they both awoke at the exact same moment, as if primed to do so. This time they could see the black bulk of something enormous standing over them, silhouetted against the night sky. It was so close they could almost touch its thick black coat.

'Oh my God,' gasped Donald.

'Don't move,' cautioned Andy.

For what seemed an eternity, they lay rigid while the beast held its ground, its head looming over them, examining them in turn. Then, quite suddenly, it turned on its heels and sloped off into the darkness.

'Do you think it followed us here?' said Donald when his trembling subsided.

'Well, at least it left our stuff alone this time,' replied Andy nervously. 'Do you think it'll be back?'

'Not now. It'll be daylight soon.' Neither was able to sleep, so Andy stoked up the remains of the fire and boiled the kettle to make tea. 'What do you think it was?' he asked Donald as he spooned sugar into his mug.

Donald shook his head. 'I reckon it's an escaped panther, or something like that. But why did it decide to leave us alone this time?' He stared hard at Andy. 'I wasn't imagining it, was I? It was pretty huge, wasn't it?'

His friend nodded. 'Colossal,' he concurred.

'Ought we to tell the ranger?'

Andy shrugged his shoulders. 'He didn't seem that interested, did he? Besides, I really don't want to go back there again. I think we should press on. We've only a day left.'

Mid-morning, the fine weather changed and a thin spray of rain washed across the parched landscape. With temperatures remaining high, however, it proved a welcome contrast from the relentless heat of the previous days. By evening, the sun had returned, casting a golden glow. By then Andy and Donald had covered some thirty miles and were freewheeling into the town of Newton Stewart.

'Let's find a hostel for tonight,' pleaded Donald. 'I don't think I'd be able to cope with another cat call. Do you know what? I could really do with a pint in a pub and a night's uninterrupted sleep.'

Andy agreed, but, finding the town hostel full, they were redirected to an inexpensive bed and breakfast close to Creebridge. 'You'll like Mrs Hannay,' the girl at the hostel told them. 'She's really easy going. Just loves her young men, she does.'

'I'm not sure I'm up to that,' quipped Andy, but was reassured when Mrs Hannay turned out to be a plump, elderly woman intent on watering a flowerbed full of delphiniums and snapdragons.

'Come ben the hoos,' she announced cheerily, escorting them into a spacious bedroom at the back of her cottage. 'Ye'll have to share, mind,' she continued. 'But it's a big enough bed.'

'Civilisation,' sighed Donald as he caught sight of the fresh linen sheets and adjoining bathroom. 'Not that it hasn't been great being out in the open, but this is paradise.'

The cottage, whitewashed with a tiled roof, was set back from the road and fringed by old trees. They deposited their bicycles in the garden shed, and their amiable landlady directed them to a pub within walking distance. It was obviously well patronised and they were soon in conversation with Archie McLellan, who introduced himself as the local historian.

'Ah, that'll be the Dark Lord,' he pronounced when they finished telling him about their experiences with the big cat.

'The Dark Lord! Do you mean it's some sort of phantom?' gasped Andy, always susceptible to ghost stories.

'Ay, that'll be right,' said Archie.

Long ago, he explained, all of the surrounding territory had

belonged to either the Stewart earls of Galloway or their neighbours, the mighty House of Douglas. The Stewarts were a notably
prolific dynasty, and, in the early eighteenth century, an earl of
Galloway had presented a black cougar as a pet to one of his
many illegitimate sons. It was a fine beast imported as a cub from
North America, and soon became so attached to its master that it
would only leave his side when he retired to bed.

Now, as it transpired, this young man had recently quarrelled
with a member of the Douglas family. Nobody remembers what
the argument was about, only that on a dark autumnal night
two armed horsemen arrived at the castle to seize the young lord
and carry him off into the darkness by force. He was never seen
again.

The cougar cub was bereft and desperately searched for its
master, eventually venturing further afield and disappearing into
the hills. He was never caught, but as the years passed he became
the stuff of legend. From sightings of a large black beast reported
at intervals over the centuries, the phantom cat eventually earned
the nickname of the Dark Lord.

'It'll be the Dark Lord you saw,' confirmed Archie confidently.
'He's still searching for his master and the two men who took
him away.'

Back at the cottage, Andy and Donald joked about Archie's
story. 'The Dark Lord must have thought our bikes were horses,'
quipped the former before falling asleep.

The softness of the mattress sent both of them into a deep,
relaxed sleep in which they dreamed of the open road and water-
falls and rolling hills. Then, all of a sudden, they were both wide
awake and paralysed with terror.

Standing at the foot of the bed was the looming hulk of the
large black cat, its yellow eyes inflamed.

'How did it get into our room?' gasped Andy, sitting up, his back pressed against the headboard. 'I thought you said you'd closed the window!'

Donald was too petrified to speak.

Once again, the two friends sat it out in an attempt to out-stare the beast. Another eternity passed before, entirely without warning, the panther turned sideways to effortlessly leap through the bedroom wall. 'My God, did you see that?' groaned Donald. 'I told you I shut the window.'

At breakfast, Mrs Hannay was highly entertained by their revelation. 'Och, dinna believe a word Archie McLellan tells you,' she said. 'It'll have been my own wee moggie you saw.'

As she spoke, a small black cat jumped onto the window seat before slipping out into the garden. 'Let's just say that I named him after the Dark Lord,' said Mrs Hannay with a wink.

21

DISTILLED SPIRITS

If a body could just find oot the exac' proper proportion and quantity that ought to be drunk every day,
and keep to that, I verily trow that he might live
forever, without dying at a', and that doctors and
kirkyards would go oot o' fashion.

James Hogg, the Ettrick Shepherd (1770–1835)

Phantom cats, poltergeists, omens, enchanted forests and ancient
curses. These old wives' tales have been around for such a long
time that there simply has to be something in them. Make fun
of them if you must, but the very fact that nobody has ever been
able entirely to disprove their credibility only serves to enhance
the fascination we all have with them.

On touring Speyside, the impression is of long expanses of
tranquil meadowland encroached upon by the passive reaches
of the River Spey as it winds its leisurely way towards the Moray
Firth. This is the heart of Scotch whisky country, the land of the
uisge beatha, the 'Water of Life.' Around every corner, and strikingly present in the intermittent small towns, are the Speyside
distilleries with their distinctive pagoda turrets. Is it any wonder

that here, more than anywhere else, the spirits of the past go hand in hand with spirits of a more liquid substance?

Access to a reliable supply of water is integral to the manufacture of Scotch whisky. More than anything, it is the proximity of water which determines the setting for a distillery. But while the Rothes Burn that flows in front of the Glenrothes Distillery, south of Elgin, provides the power to harness its water wheel, the water for the stills needs to be as pure and cold as possible.

Luckily there have always been ample supplies in the hills upstream, bubbling up through the granite rocks to emerge in a series of springs and wells. Among these sources is the Fairies' Well, allegedly the scene of a gruesome double murder at the end of the fourteenth century.

When the Fairies' Well became a water source for Glenrothes a hundred or so years ago, it connected the distillery directly to one of the most enduring legends of Speyside. The story centres around the now ruined Castle of Rothes, then home to Sir Andrew Leslie.

Sir Andrew's daughter Mary was extremely beautiful and excited the interest of the notorious Alexander Stewart, the King's Lieutenant in the Highlands, who later, for his various nefarious deeds, became known as 'the Wolf of Badenoch'.

Stewart soon realised he had competition for the lady's hand in the form of Malcolm Grant, master of nearby Arndilly, who had recently returned from a crusade to the Holy Land. As long as Grant was on the scene, Stewart's efforts to win Mary's heart would come to nothing, so he decided to imprison his rival at his Castle of Lochindorb. When Grant escaped, Stewart decided to have him killed.

The chosen assassin was Stewart's attendant, a grotesque-looking dwarf known as 'The Hawk', who followed the two lovers on an evening stroll beside the Rothes Burn. When they reached the Fairies' Well and sat down for a rest, the Hawk crept up from behind and stabbed Grant with his *sgean dubh*. He was about to use his dagger again when Mary Leslie leapt in between them and caught the blow. When the couple were discovered dead the next day, they were seen to be locked in each other's arms beneath a bush that had grown up overnight.

Thereafter, it is claimed, the bush only breaks into leaf on the anniversary of their deaths. Today, a small monument commemorating the legend stands opposite the Glenrothes Distillery beside the Rothes cemetery where the couple were supposedly interred.

Whether this anecdote is to be believed or not, the Rothes kirkyard is undoubtedly the resting place of Biawa, one of the town's favourite sons and also its most unlikely resident.

Biawa, who died in 1972, had lived in Rothes from the end of the nineteenth century, when he was brought to Scotland from his native Africa by Major James Grant, owner of the Glen Grant distillery. Grant had been on safari and had come across the boy, then aged about ten, abandoned by the wayside – hence the name he was given.

After efforts to trace his parents had failed, Major Grant decided to adopt Biawa as one of his servants. He started off as the major's pageboy, served in the First World War and, at some point afterwards, played for his local football club, Rothes FC. It must have made the town appear very exotic to visiting players. There were not many soccer teams in Scotland with an African butler for a goalie.

When the major died in 1931, he left Biawa the sum of £200 and instructed his heirs at Glen Grant House to retain him as a servant, 'so long as he is obedient, respectful and willing to remain'. By all accounts, Biawa was a quiet soul whose one passion was Rothes FC, where he was given a complementary seat for life and a cup of tea at half-time whenever there was a match. Biawa's contact with the Glenrothes Distillery was through those who worked there, and among these was Paul Rickards, who remembers him as an old man with long grey hair and a beard which gave him an uncanny resemblance to the Arthurian wizard Merlin.

Paul was later put in charge of spirit quality at the Scotch whisky blenders Robertson & Baxter, a job which involved regular visits to distilleries, at least once or twice a year. On one such trip to Glenrothes in 1979, the stillman took him aside and warned him that 'a presence' had been seen in the newly built still-house.

'He and several others had noticed an old, dark-skinned man with a straggly grey beard during the evening and night shifts,' said Paul. 'When he described him, I knew exactly who he was talking about.'

Seven years after Biawa's death, his spirit had obviously been disturbed.

On returning home to Glasgow, Paul contacted Cedric Wilson, a professor of pharmacology who he knew had an interest in the paranormal. Professor Wilson was keen to find out more, and, as soon as permission had been obtained, the two men drove to Speyside to visit the distillery.

It was over a weekend in the summer, and the distillery was closed for the silent season. After spending a morning on his own in the still-house, Professor Wilson concluded that the problem originated from the ancient ley lines which run under the foundations of the new building. Ley lines, which in the Chinese culture of feng shui are known as 'dragon currents', are made up of a series of supernatural pathways connecting with preordained sacred sites. From Rothes Castle, for example, these spiritual alignments run northwards through Rothes cemetery, and onwards to the old Pictish capital of Burghhead on the Moray Firth.

The professor was absolutely convinced that Biawa's spirit had been agitated when the foundations were excavated. Moreover, it was unlikely to be at peace until the magnetic force of the mystical currents had been restored. He therefore recommended that two stakes of scrap 'pig iron' be driven into the ground on either side of the still-house.

What happened next convinced Paul that the professor was on to something. 'He walked straight over to Biawa's grave and said a few words in the form of a blessing.'

How Professor Wilson knew exactly where to look for Biawa's last resting place among the hundreds of nondescript tombstones that crowd the terraced slopes of the Rothes Cemetery remains a complete mystery. But whatever strange forces were at work on that day, no more ghosts have since been seen at the Glenrothes Distillery, and Biawa, the loyal servant and Rothes Football Club supporter, appears to have now found lasting peace.

A former distillery manager who definitely failed to find lasting peace, however, was Duncan MacCallum of the Campbeltown distillery of Glen Scotia on Kintyre. A member of the West Highland Malt Distillers' Society, which he helped to found in 1919, Duncan fell into such a deep depression when Glen Scotia closed in 1928 that he drowned himself in Cambeltown Loch. The distillery reopened in the late 1980s, and his lonely spectral figure has been a regular visitor ever since.

Over on the far side of the country, in Aberdeenshire, the Glendronach Distillery near Huntly features a far more exotic resident, who was first encountered by one of the distillery's warehousemen over thirty years ago.

Glendronach's original distillery building was destroyed by a fire some ten years after it opened. Since then, it has been rebuilt, resurrected, closed, rescued again in 1920 and mothballed until finally reopening in 2004. Since 2008 it has been independently owned by the Benriach Distillery Company Limited, but it was under an earlier ownership that sightings of a Spanish flamenco dancer began.

Those who know about Scotch whisky will be well aware that several factors influence its individual taste and character, not least the type of barrel in which the spirit is left to mature. At Glendronach Distillery, a large number of Oloroso sherry casks were imported for that purpose during the 1970s.

And it was while one such shipment was being unloaded from a lorry that a mysterious stowaway was spotted escaping from one of the empty casks. Small and dark, she was later described as wearing a scarlet and black Spanish costume with a full mantilla.

Of course, that was by no means the end of the matter. Since that day there have been numerous reports of a dark-haired beauty lurking in the shadows of the Glendronach warehouse, or seen moving swiftly through the still-house, her skirts rustling alongside the distillery's distinctive pagoda-headed malt kiln.

It has even been suggested that she has taken up residence at the nearby Glen House, which the distillery owns. Built in the eighteenth century, Glen House provides twelve guest rooms for distillery visitors. On a number of occasions, single gentlemen staying overnight have experienced an unexpected, although seemingly not at all unpleasant, visitation in the night.

22

THE SLEEPING BEAUTY

'She sits on the rock alone. Her head bends on her arm of snow. Her dark hair is in the wind. Hear, son of Fingal, her song, it is smooth as the gliding stream.' We came to the silent bay, and heard the maid of night.

James Macpherson, *The Poems of Ossian* (1773)

It had been raining for days on end. But then it always rains in Scotland, Naomi told herself. There were times when she felt she was living in a car wash. It had been months since she remembered seeing a ray of sunlight through the clouds, but possibly that was only because of her mood of resentment. She could barely remember a time when Ewan had walked in and out of the front door without an umbrella.

Ewan and Naomi Lockhart had been married for six years. He belonged to an old-established Edinburgh legal family; she was born and brought up in Yorkshire. They had met at a mutual friend's wedding in Harrogate and, following a frenzied courtship largely conducted over weekends, they had married and set up home together in Edinburgh's New Town, where Ewan worked for a venture capital fund.

On Naomi's part, it had involved a major adjustment to penetrate the tight social circles her husband had been accustomed to since birth. It had certainly not been easy. With the combinations of shared education and childhood parties, Ewan's friends formed a solid, self-reliant and, some might observe, self-satisfied clique, suspicious of outsiders. Unfamiliar with the colloquial names and places to which they constantly referred, Naomi often felt excluded from their incestuous jokes and petty squabbles. There was too much shared past history from which she felt shut out. Sometimes, she suspected they only tolerated her because she was Ewan's other half. When she mentioned this to him, he laughed and told her not to be so paranoid. 'It'll be different when we have kids,' he insisted.

That, of course, was part of the problem. They had been trying since their wedding night, but as the weeks and months passed, it began to look as if there might be a problem. Doctors were consulted – Edinburgh is well served with paediatricians and experts on pregnancy – but the tests showed nothing obviously wrong. 'Keep trying,' was the medical verdict.

While Ewan worked long hours, with trips abroad to meet up with clients, Naomi took a part-time job with an estate agent, supervising valuations. As she thumbed through the property brochures, she dreamily reassured herself that she was happy enough with her lot.

Then, one day, she came across it: 'Island of Lewis. Tigh na Hag. Hebridean croft for sale. Spectacular coastal location. Two bedrooms. In need of renovation. Six acres of land.'

The accompanying image showed an oblong, whitewashed one-storey villa on a hillside with a glimpse of sea beyond. Against the backdrop of an azure sky, it looked idyllic. And so incredibly cheap.

Ewan's reaction was more cautious. 'If we're going to invest in a holiday cottage, wouldn't you rather go to the sun – Spain or the Algarve? It's very cut off up there.'

'But isn't that exactly what we need?' pleaded Naomi. 'To get away to somewhere on our own whenever we feel the urge?'

What she did not say was that it would be away from his parents and his friends who constantly, if unintentionally, reminded her that they were childless. 'It looks so beautiful and I know we can afford it,' she pleaded. 'It's also not that difficult to get to. I've checked it out. Just think, we could drive up for weekends. There are ferry crossings from Uig on Skye and Ullapool on the mainland, and daily flights to Stornoway from Edinburgh and Glasgow airports.'

Ewan was unconvinced. 'If that's what you want, I'll look into it,' he told her.

The island of Lewis is a place where the treeless, sponge-like earth meets the sky. From the moment Naomi set eyes on Tigh na Hag, it was love at first sight. It also chanced to be one of those gloriously clear spring afternoons when the sun-soaked moor of peat and heather glowed the colour of biscuit and grape.

'Just look at that view,' Naomi enthused as they stepped out of the Callanish Visitor Centre. 'Come on, Ewan, I'm going to hug a stone.'

They had hired a car at Stornoway Airport and, having inspected Tigh na Hag, which they both agreed was a bargain, dis-covered that the ancient megalithic standing stones of Callanish were within a couple of miles' walking distance. As they strolled gently up the paved pathway towards the circle of stones, a black and white collie dog bounded over to greet them.

'Good boy,' said Naomi, assuming it was male and patting him on the back. The dog wagged his tail and dribbled before disappearing behind a fence.

'You shouldn't encourage stray dogs,' said Ewan. 'You don't know who he belongs to.'

Naomi ignored him. Nothing could spoil her happiness as she reached forward to run her hands over the smooth pinkish surface of the nearest standing stone. 'Aren't they incredible?' she said. 'It says in the guidebook they were transported here from somewhere up the coast near enough five thousand years ago. Nobody knows how or why.'

'It's because of the Sleeping Beauty,' interrupted a voice, and behind them stood a dark-skinned man with the density of jet-black hair usually only found in Spain. He was slim, wearing faded jeans underneath an equally well-worn anorak. Naomi judged he must be in his mid-thirties.

'If you look over there at that mountain range to the south-west, you'll see it resembles the body of a reclining woman with her hair cascading over her shoulders and breasts.'

Ewan smiled cynically, but Naomi was intrigued. 'I suppose so,' she said, screwing up her eyes in the sunlight. 'But what has that to do with the stones?'

The man approached and stood close enough for her to notice his startling sky-blue eyes, so different from the indecisive grey-green of her husband's. His face was stippled with stubble, suggesting either vanity or laziness. Unaware of the discomfort his physicality was causing, he unintentionally pressed against her.

'The standing stones here are aligned to the moon,' he continued and she noted a trace of Gaelic in his accent. 'Seven times a century, the moon stands still on the summer solstice. If you stand where you are standing now, you will witness the new moon rise from the womb of the Sleeping Beauty, as if she is giving birth.'

'What a load of nonsense,' said Ewan when he and Naomi returned to the car park. Naomi glanced sideways at her husband.

Sometimes she despaired of him. He was such a spoilsport. Somehow it made her all the more determined to buy the croft.

On reaching the road junction, the black and white collie raced ahead of them towards Carloway village, where they were to stay the night. 'Isn't that the dog we saw earlier?' she said.

'Perhaps he belongs to your anorak friend?' suggested Ewan.

It was not until the middle of the following year that the Lockharts returned, catching the evening ferry from Uig on Skye to Tarbert on Harris. With their hired van stuffed to capacity with the basics of furniture, food, utilities and bedding, it was not until darkness fell that they arrived at Tigh na Hag. 'Bad timing,' said Ewan. 'We should have booked into a B&B for the night.'

'Oh, we'll manage,' said Naomi, unlocking the front door. 'Isn't this fun? You bring in the sleeping bags and I'll brew us a pot of tea.'

Away from Edinburgh, she felt free to be herself, liberated from the dreary round of Ewan's friends, the cocktail parties and candle-lit suppers. This deserted cottage was what she had dreamed of. This was where she and Ewan would conceive their first child.

Fortunately, they had brought torches and a couple of butane lanterns with them. The interior was dry, and it did not take long for them to make themselves comfortable. Exhausted, they curled up in sleeping bags and fell instantly asleep.

It was making the croft habitable that preoccupied their daylight hours over the ensuing weekend. Having purchased a ladder in Stornoway, Ewan clambered onto the roof to inspect the state of the slate tiles, while Naomi scrubbed the stone floor and draped oversized curtains across windows. 'We'll need to paint the frames,' she informed Ewan.

So preoccupied did they become with their basic chores that the upsets and differences of Edinburgh rapidly evaporated. Their time on Lewis was measured by the hours of daylight. For a full five days, they saw only one another. Then the black and white collie dog came to call.

Ewan had set off early that morning to find out if there was trout fishing on one or other of the lochs nearby. Naomi had stayed behind to sun herself in a deck chair on the front doorstep when the dog ran up to her, breathing heavily. 'Hello, boy!' she said, patting him on the head. 'Where did you come from?'

The dog gazed up at her in a friendly manner and rubbed his head against her leg before disappearing behind the croft. Moments later, the stranger arrived.

'Are you looking for your dog? He went in that direction,' said Naomi, gesturing towards the rear of the building.

'So you're back,' said the man. Once again she was struck by the sky-blue of his eyes. 'My name's Calum MacLeod,' he added.

'Naomi Lockhart,' she responded with a broad smile. He was rather handsome, she confirmed to herself.

'I see you've been fixing up the old croft,' Calum observed approvingly.

'Yes, it's quite a challenge, but we love it. Do you live nearby?'

'Over there.' He pointed vaguely to the south-west.

'Beside the Sleeping Beauty?' she found herself asking and, for some inexplicable reason, felt the colour rush to her cheeks.

'That'll be right,' he said, not letting on if he had noticed. 'Remember the morrow's the solstice.'

'I'd completely forgotten,' she lied. She was not entirely sure what the solstice was, or why it was significant.

Calum nodded, raised his hand in a cheerful salute and set off.

Naomi watched him as he did so, his long athletic legs striding purposefully over the uneven turf. 'Don't forget your dog,' she called after him.

When Ewan returned, she told him they had had their very first visitor. 'I hope he doesn't become a nuisance,' he said dismissively.

'That's not very friendly. He was only being neighbourly. He came to tell me it's the solstice tomorrow.'

'What a chancer,' chided her husband. 'All that lunar nonsense. He must fancy you.'

'Don't be ridiculous,' Naomi retorted, her face reddening. 'If I didn't know you better, I'd think you were jealous!'

Ewan laughed and snapped open a can of lager.

The next day dawned fine and clear, and Ewan, having made contact with the landowner, passed an idyllic day with his fishing rod on a nearby lochan. In the late afternoon he returned to the croft having landed a dozen medium-sized silver trout by mid-afternoon. That evening, regardless of midges, they sat outside and shared a bottle of Chablis.

'Are you coming with me to the standing stones tonight?' asked Naomi.

'You must be joking,' snorted Ewan, pulling a face. 'If you're going to go in for all that New Age nonsense, you're on your own, girl.'

How infuriating it is when a good mood is deliberately spoiled, reflected Naomi as the indignation swelled up inside her. 'All right then, I'll go on my own,' she snapped and stormed indoors to change her clothes. Ewan remained indifferent.

It was after ten o'clock and still light outside. Stuff Ewan, she thought to herself. He had been off on his own all day having a rare old time while she had been left behind to clean up the mess he had made in the kichen. Tonight, she was going to do something she wanted to do for herself. Nothing and no one was going to stop her. She loved Ewan, but there were times – and this was one of them – when she wondered why she had married him.

Having made the decision to go to the standing stones on her own, Naomi grabbed a torch from beside the front door. 'Don't wait up for me,' she called out as she departed.

Beneath her feet the ground was alternately rough and spongy, and she cursed her sandals for their ineffectual protection. There was still enough light for her to make out the recognisable outlines of the landscape. As she approached Callanish, she turned round to admire the far-off silhouette of the Sleeping Beauty mountain range sketched inkily against a steely sky.

And then she fell over, her body succumbing to the soft springy undergrowth underneath her. She giggled, blaming it on the third glass of Chablis.

So far as Naomi Lockhart was concerned, what took place over the following six hours remains a complete blank in her memory. As she lay flat on her back against a soft bed of heather and peat, peaceful and strangely unperturbed by her predicament, she heard heavy breathing and felt the wet sensation of a rough tongue licking her face.

It was the collie dog. His breath smelled unexpectedly sweet, and his presence was curiously comforting. Very gently, he lay down on the turf beside her with his head on her shoulder.

How long they remained there under the night stars she could later not recall, only that the dog kept her company as the new moon catapulted into the heavens. At long last, almost too soon, the dawn broke and Naomi awoke to find herself alone.

Surprised by an overwhelming feeling of well-being, not to mention the realisation that her ankle no longer throbbed, Naomi returned to Tigh na Hag where she found Ewan snoring in their bed.

'How did you get on with your summer soltice?' he asked her as they packed up the van that afternoon.

'Unforgettable,' she announced, smiling to herself.

Ewan and Naomi Lockhart have returned to Tigh na Hag every summer since that first holiday. Sometimes, when Ewan's work allows, they go in the autumn and early spring. Eight months to the day of that first Summer Solstice at Callanish, Naomi gave birth to Mhairi, their first daughter, a strikingly beautiful child conspicuous for her jet-black hair and sky-blue eyes.

23

OMENS AND CURSES

This belief in a race of little men is common to most island folk, and they are the direct ancestors of the gremlins invented by the Air Force during the last war as a way of accounting for any unexpected misfortune.

Douglas Sutherland, *Against the Wind* (1966)

Harbingers of doom are intertwined with the culture of the Celt. Mock them at your peril. On the Isle of Arran, the birth of a white stag heralds the demise of a duke of Hamilton; a ghostly galleon is seen on Loch Fyne before a duke of Argyll faces mortality; a decapitated horseman known as Ewen of the Little Head warns of impending death in the Clan MacEwen on Mull; an orb of light hovers over Loch Linnhe when the death of a Stewart is imminent.

At Barnbougle Castle on the Dalmeny estate at South Queensferry, a mysterious hound is said to howl through the night as an earl of Rosebery approaches his end. A story then unfolds from the twelfth century, when the castle's owner was one Sir Roger de Moubray, who had gone to the Holy Land to fight in a crusade. His favourite dog was left behind to guard Barnbougle in his absence and on the very night that its master was struck down in a foreign land, the disconsolate beast was heard to bay inconsolably for hours on end.

Everybody knows the apocryphal tale of how a saltire of white cloud miraculously appeared in the sky before the Battle of Athelstaneford. Hardly anyone noticed when a similar phenomenon occurred during the International Gathering of the Clans at Holyrood in 2009. An omen to do with Scottish independence? We shall have to wait and see.

Superstition is the oxygen of the supernatural. Talismans, lucks and crystals are its tools. In *Supernatural Scotland* I wrote about the Colstoun Pear, the Lee Penny and the Faerie Flag of Dunvegan. But there are other contenders.

The Glenorchy Charmstone, a polished pyramid of rock crystal, was picked up on the Greek island of Rhodes during a battle with the Turks. Today, it sits safely in the National Museums of Scotland, alongside the Clach na Bratach, an unmounted ball of rock associated with the Jacobite Clan Donnachaidh. When a flaw in the latter appeared in it the night before the Battle of Sheriffmuir, the Jacobites lost.

Dipped in water, the healing properties of the Clach Dearg, or Red Stone, which belongs to the Stewarts of Ardvorlich, became so famous in the Victorian era that people came from all over the world to seek cures for skin diseases and liver complaints. I am surprised that nobody has thought of bottling it.

Curses are efficacious because people genuinely want to believe in them, whether they admit to it or not. Thankfully, most of the ones we know about were set in motion a long time ago, so there are few surprises when they come back to haunt us.

The MacAlisters of Kintyre descend from the mighty Somerled, a fearsome warlord who led the Gaels to victory against Norway. The clan has occupied Loop and Glenbarr on the Kintyre Peninsula for centuries, but at one time held Ardpatrick at the entrance to West Loch Tarbert. And it was here that the Curse of MacAlister came to its climax.

During a skirmish in the seventeenth century, MacAlister Mor took prisoner the two sons of a widow and, despite her entreaties, hanged them both from a gibbet in front of her door. As the victims gasped their last, their heartbroken mother turned angrily upon MacAlister Mor and cried out, 'The House of MacAlister Mor shall have no more sons.' And so it came to pass.

For 100 years, only daughters were born to the Chiefly House of MacAlister. Then to the universal joy of the clan, a son was born at last.

The boy grew up and married, but when the Jacobites rebelled against the government in 1715, the Younger of MacAlister rode off to enlist with them at Perth. Months passed without a word from him until late one night the household was awoken by the sound of a horse entering the courtyard. The horse was riderless and when it reached the front door, it fell down dead.

Overjoyed, the young Mrs MacAlister waited in her bedroom for her husband's return, but when the door swung open there stood before her a headless man.

A brief and indecisive battle had taken place at Sheriffmuir. The young MacAlister had been captured, put on trial for treason and executed. With the stroke of an axe, the Chiefly line of MacAlister Mor passed to a distant kinsman.

The hamlet of Glenuig in the West Lochaber parish of Morar is a popular destination for hill-walkers and sea kayakers. Close by is the 200-year-old crofting community of Smirisary, where many of the dwellings have been renovated, and it was in one of these that the sculptor Andrew Kinghorn found himself staying one summer.

Creative, but certainly not suggestible, Andrew had set off to explore the rocky foreshore, but on returning to the croft was gripped by the most terrifying feeling of pure evil.

When he discussed this with his friends who owned the croft, they remembered being told that the next-door croft had fallen into ruin when its occupant had failed to return from the market. He had gone there to sell his beasts, and it was rumoured that he had been robbed and murdered. Allegedly, his killer also came from Smirisary, and the crofter had cursed him with his dying breath.

Admirers of Sir Henry Raeburn's iconic portrait of Colonel Alastair Ranaldson Macdonell of Glengarry in the Scottish National Portrait Gallery in Edinburgh rarely associate this handsome, plaid-clad figure with the remote and empty glens of Knoydart on the Sound of Sleat.

Macdonell inherited his estates aged nineteen and squandered his inheritance. By the time he met his death leaping from a canal steamer in 1828, he was virtually bankrupt. As a result, Aeneas, his son, was obliged to sell the Glengarry estates, but he managed to retain Knoydart. Still unable to make ends meet, however, he emigrated to Australia in 1840; it was not a success, and after two years had passed he returned to Knoydart. He died at Inverie in 1852. It was then that the situation really became fraught.

In 1853, Alastair, the colonel's eldest grandson, inherited Knoydart under-age and, pressured by his mother Josephine, allowed the 17,500-acre estate to be sold to pay off family debts. For the incumbent crofters, it was a catastrophe.

Many of them were substantially in arrears with their rent and, with the blessing of the British Government, the land was cleared for sheep farming. In 1852, 400 crofting tenants at Knoydart were evicted and, as compensation, offered passage to Canada and Australia. Few of them wanted to go, but, being landless and poverty-stricken, they had no option.

On 17 September 1853, the *Sillery*, bound for Nova Scotia, weighed anchor off the Isle of Oronsay. An eye-witness observed that, 'The wail of the poor women and children as they were torn away from their homes would have melted a heart of stone.'

Apparently not the heart of Josephine Macdonell, who had come with her factor to witness the evacuation. Those who refused to go quietly saw their homes set alight and levelled to the ground.

In 1997, the Knoydart Foundation was established by Highland Council in partnership with the local community, the Chris Brasher Trust, the Kilchoan estate, and the John Muir Trust. A new pier was installed in 2006, and self-catering tourism, appealing to those drawn by the isolation and intense beauty of the landscape, has developed into the principal source of local income.

Staying at Inverie, Andrea Forbes from Pollokshaws was conscious of an overwhelming sensation of sadness as she approached by motorboat. 'I may just have been imagining it,' she said. 'But it all started when we saw that amazing white statue of the Virgin Mary rising from the hillside overlooking the loch. It made me think that she must have been placed there to symbolise atonement.'

As you sow, so shall you reap. The curses on the Chiefly House of Macdonell cannot be rejected lightly.

In 1855, Aeneas, Josephine's second son, died in a drowning accident at the age of twenty. In 1857, Alastair, seventeenth Chief of Macdonell, sailed for New Zealand, where he died of rheumatic fever at the early age of twenty-eight.

Having also emigrated to New Zealand, Josephine's third son Charles became the eighteenth Chief in 1862. He died at sea six years later, aged thirty-two.

After this, the Macdonell Chiefship passed to a cousin. By then the headland and glens of Knoydart lay deserted, silent and haunted forever.

24

PALIMPSEST

There is a great deal to be said,
For being dead.

Edmund Clerihew Bentley,
'Biography for Beginners' (1905)

As the moon revolves around the earth and the earth circum-navigates the sun, the great clock of our short existence measures out our lives. Seasons and centuries come and go in the pitiless marathon of time. There is nothing to hold onto but the past as we are swept along into the passage of eternity.

In the process of writing *Haunted Scotland* and its predecessor, *Supernatural Scotland*, I have vigorously interrogated almost everyone I know on the subject of the paranormal. For this I ask their forgiveness but, having done so, I am still not sure that I am personally any the wiser.

Ghosts, phantoms, poltergeists, time-slips, second sight, reincarnation, witchcraft, curses, demons and guardian angels, tales of terror and dread have been handed down from father to son, from mother to daughter. There is nothing we enjoy more than jumping at our own shadows. It seems that our appetite for dread of the unknown is insatiable.

Yet why should we be alarmed by the intangible? If there is nothing there, there is nothing to fear. If there is something there, it has to be there for a reason.

And if we fail to take a grip on our imaginations we can end up in all kinds of trouble, literally frightening ourselves to death.

Consider, for example, an event which took place in the autumn of 1810, when 326 cavalry officers, 800 artillery, and 1,158 infantrymen were stationed in an army camp beside the town of Haddington, in East Lothian.

Among the first to occupy the barracks were the 25th, or Sussex Regiment, and it was a trivial dispute between two of its officers, Captain Hugh Blair Rutherford and Doctor Cahill, that led to the ensuing tragedy.

Although nobody could remember afterwards what the two men had quarrelled about, neither was prepared to back down for fear of loss of face. A duel was therefore fought and the twenty-four-year-old Captain Rutherford mortally wounded. Great remorse was shown over his demise, and his funeral, which took place in the graveyard of St Martin's Chapel in Haddington, was largely attended.

St Martin's Chapel, it should be explained, was located in close proximity to the army barracks and although it had been largely destroyed during the Reformation, its graveyard was where the soldiers were then interred when they died of either natural causes or sheer tedium.

Greatly distressed, Captain Rutherford's fellow officers congregated after the burial to discuss what had occurred. Copious quantities of wine were consumed and a ghoulish wager struck in which Lieutenant Gray, infuriated that his close friend had risen to the challenge in the first place, agreed to return to the graveyard at midnight to plunge his dagger into his comrade's grave in protest.

Wrapped in a large military cloak, the lieutenant set off into the night. Hours passed until eventually his friends, becoming concerned as to his welfare, went in search of him. As they crossed the River Tyne, the black silhouette of the ruined chapel loomed against the monochrome sky. They could see no sign of movement but when they entered the graveyard with their torches, they found Lieutenant Gray's lifeless body hunched over their comrade's burial plot.

What was even more terrifying was that when they attempted to lift him, his body refused to budge. It was as if it had been stapled to the ground.

And only then did it become apparent that the intoxicated Gray had plunged his dagger into the ground up to the hilt through the material of his cloak. In his agitation, the young lieutenant had inadvertently skewered himself onto the ground and, in so doing, convinced himself that he was being held down by some supernatural power. Despite his young age, the shock had caused him to have a massive heart attack.

Or had it? We shall never know. Today, the burial ground of St Martin's Chapel, flanked by Whittingehame Drive and overlooked by the modern housing of Bullet Loan, has long vanished beneath a swathe of grass. On the hour of midnight, nevertheless, a cloaked figure has from time to time been sighted vanishing into the roofless chapel choir.

All of us are susceptible to fear, but God forbid we share the fate of the luckless Lieutenant Gray. Fear, however, is what encourages us to search for reasons beyond our reach; to provide rational explanations for the irrational; to give names to the shadows in the gloom. Inevitably, I have strayed into territories in my research that I would have preferred not to. If trifled with, the realms of parapsychology and the psychic can be exceedingly dangerous.

Once the imagination kicks into play, its inventive power is unlimited and irrevocable. It is irresponsible to trifle with fragility. Telepathy moves objects; transfers thought and bends metal. Willpower transcends opposition.

One day science will reveal all, but until then it is important to retain an intelligent equilibrium on the subject. A sense of humour also helps, if only to lighten the burden.

Scotland, as I observed earlier, lends itself uncompromisingly to the occult and paranormal. Superstition is embedded deep in our multicultural, multi-faith psyche. In my investigations I have attempted to remain non-judgemental throughout, allowing anecdotes and incidents to speak for themselves, and throwing in a few of my own encounters with the inexplicable.

But if I have discovered anything on my adventures it is that answers are elusive. Opinions are contradictory. After at least 3,000 years of human intelligence, nobody has as yet successfully made the breakthrough into the conundrum of parallel worlds.

BIBLIOGRAPHY

Armour, Mary. *Helen Duncan, My Living Has Not Been In Vain – A story of Helen's life and work,* Pembridge Publishing, 2000.

Barnett, T. Ratcliffe, *Border By-Ways and Lothian Lore,* John Grant Booksellers, 1944.

Booth, M., *A Magick Life: The Life of Aleister Crowley,* Coronet Books, 2001.

Campbell, Harry, *Supernatural Scotland (Scottish Collection),* Collins, 1999.

Campbell, John Lorne, *Strange Things: The Story of Dr Allan McDonald, Ada Goodrich Freer, And the Society for Psychological Research's Enquiry into Highland Second Sight,* Birlinn, 2006.

Coghill, Hamish, *Lost Edinburgh,* Birlinn, 2008.

Coventry, Martin, *Haunted Houses and Castles in Scotland,* Goblinshead, 2004. *A Wee Guide to Scottish Ghosts and Bogles,* Goblinshead, 2004.

Crowley, Aleister, *The Confessions of Aleister Crowley,* Routledge & Kegan Paul, 1979.

Gordon, Seton, *Highways and Byways in the West Highlands,* Macmillan, 1935.

Henderson, Jan-Andrew, *The Ghost That Haunted Itself – the Story of the Mackenzie Poltergeist,* Mainstream Publishing, 2001.

Henderson, Lizanne & Cowan, Professor Edward, *Scottish Fairy Belief,* Tuckwell Pess, 2001.

Love, Dane, *Scottish Ghosts*, Robert Hale, 2003.

Martine, Roddy, *Supernatural Scotland*, Robert Hale, 2003.

McCormick, Donald, *The Mystery of Lord Kitchener's Death*, Putnam, 1959.

Neil, Arnold (Foreword by Dr Karl Shuker), *Monster! The A–Z of Zooform Phenomena*, CTZ, 2007.

Pugh, Roy J.M, *The Deil's Ain – The Story of Witch Prosecution in Scotland*, Harlaw Heritage, 2001.

Rodger, Charles, *The Modern Scottish Minstrel; or The Songs of Scotland of the Past Half-century with Memoirs of the Poets and Specimens in English verse of Modern Gaelic Bards*, Adam & Black, 1856.

Seafield, Lily, *Scottish Ghosts*, Pelican Publishing Co, 2001.

Smith, Jill, *The Callanish Dance – the Cycle of the Year Celebrated in the Sacred Landscape of the Western Isles*, Capall Bann Publishing, 2000.

Stewart, A.J., *Falcon – The Autobiography of his Grace James the IV, King of Scots*, Peter Davies, 1970, republished as *King's Memory* by Stuart Titles, 1988.

Sutherland, Elizabeth, *Ravens and Black Rain – The Story of Highland Second Sight*, Constable, 1985.

Turnbull, Michael T., *The Edinburgh Graveyard Guide – A Spooky Saunter through Edinburgh's Chilling Cemeteries*, Scottish Cultural, 2006.

Wilson, Alan J.; Brogan, Des & McGrail, Frank, *Ghostly Tales and Sinister Stories of Old Edinburgh*, Mainstream Publishing, 1991.

INDEX